All That I Have Not Made
Poems
1957-2020

All That I Have Not Made

Poems

1957-2020

Robert Sward

First Edition

Hidden Brook Press
www.HiddenBrookPress.com
writers@HiddenBrookPress.com

All That I Have Not Made: Poems: 1957-2020
by Robert Sward

Editor – John B. Lee
Cover Art – "The Reader", Ceramic, 2018 – Coeleen Kiebert
Cover Photo – Paul Schraub
Cover Design – Richard M. Grove
Layout and Design – Richard M. Grove

Typeset in Garamond
Printed and bound in USA
Distributed in USA by Ingram
in Canada by Hidden Brook Distribution

Library and Archives Canada Cataloguing in Publication

Title: All that I have not made : poems, 1957-2020 / Robert Sward.
Other titles: Poems. Selections (2020)
Names: Sward, Robert, 1933- author.
Identifiers: Canadiana 2020025409X | ISBN 9781989786024 (softcover)
Classification: LCC PS8587.W35 A6 2020 | DDC C811/.54—dc23

Gloria in Excelsis

Glory in the highest

This book is dedicated to my children:
Cheryl, Kamala, Michael, Hannah, Nicholas
and grandchildren
Aaron, Robin, Maxine, Heron, Fjord, Cygnet

Acknowledgements:

With thanks to Elissa Alford, Heidi Alford, Jonathan, Anki Alford, David Alpaugh, Charles Atkinson, Ellen Bass, Rose Black, Robert Bly, Wallace Boss, Rabbi Eli Cohen, Mark Cull, Catherine Cury, Terri Drake, Dion Farquhar, Jack Foley, Kate Gale, Dana Gioia, Heidi Alford Jones, Marty Gervais, Peter Gilford, James D. Houston, Dr. Ed Jackson, Stephen Kessler, Coeleen Kiebert, Allan Kornblum, John B. Lee, Patrick McCarthy, Mort Marcus, Marti Mariette, Milissa Martin, Bruce Myer, William Minor, Maggie Paul, Roxi Power, Lily Rich, Psy.D, Tilly Shaw, David Swanger, Hannah Davi Sward, and J.J. Webb.

I wish to thank the Djerassi Foundation, the Edward MacDowell Association, Yaddo, the Cultural Council of Santa Cruz County, the John Simon Guggenheim Memorial Foundation, and the Canada Council for affording me an opportunity to complete this book.

Table of Contents

Uncle Dog & Other Poems, 1962

Kissing the Dancer, 1964

Thousand-Year-Old Fiancée & Other Poems, 1965

Five Iowa Poems, 1975

Movies: Left to Right, 1983

Half A Life's History, 1983

Poet Santa Cruz, 1985

Four Incarnations, 1991

from Family—A Miscellany

Sex & TV with Aunt Miriam, 1945

From Heavenly Sex, 2002

God is in The Cracks, A Narrative in Voices, 2006

ii – Jew Overboard

iii – Marriage 1, 2, 3, 4

iv – Feet Know the Way to the Other World

v – After the Bypass

New Poems

iii – Companion Animals

iv – Dr. Sward's Cure for Melancholia

Author's Note

As Jack Foley, poet and San Francisco Bay Area broadcaster puts it, "Sward moved to Canada in 1969 to take up a position as Poet-in-Residence at the University of Victoria. While there he began to practice yoga, started a publishing company (Soft Press), met and for 12 years was married to a Montreal painter.

"Indeed, two of his children are Canadian as is Sward himself—in truth, a citizen, at heart of both countries. At once a Canadian *and* American poet, one with a foot in both worlds, Sward also inhabits an enormous in-between." Or, as Rainer Maria Rilke puts it, "Every artist is born in an alien country; he has a homeland nowhere but within his own borders." (Jack Foley in *Wikipedia.)*

Harvest Time

Now in my 80s I don't feel especially old, but my life's work has been, and continues to be, poetry and, sixty years after my first publication, *Uncle Dog & Other Poems*, Putnam, London, 1957, this is harvest time. From the hundreds of poems I've written since the 1950s, these are the ones I'd like to preserve.

Because it draws on some earlier collections, *Half A Life's History: New & Selected, 1957-1983; Four Incarnations, New & Selected, 1957-1991;* and *Heavenly Sex*, (among others), I have come to think of this volume as something of a 'Collected Selected.' However, I have included twenty or so new poems as well, among them the "Dr. Sward's Cure for Melancholia" sequence (largely in my father's voice).

So, yes, this is Harvest Time. Harvest Time, or, as some would have it, End Time, Pandemic Time...

Iowa

Who would have thought, fellow writers at the Iowa Writers' Workshop, World War II and Korean War veterans like myself, aspiring poets, novelists and short story writers, the fortunate few…
A strangely innocent time, or so it seemed…

Iowa

What a strange happiness.
Sixty poets have gone off drunken, weeping into the hills.
I among them.
There is no one of us who is not a fool,
What is to be found there? ·
What is the point in this?
Someone scrawls six lines and says them.
What a strange happiness.

I think of my late wife, Gloria, struggling for ten years with Alzheimers, saying, days before her passing "I'm in the upper ten percent of the luckiest people on earth."

Amen. Amen. Me too!

"I eat the words that remain,
and am eaten. By nothing,
by all that I have not made."

—from *All For A Day*

Uncle Dog & Other Poems

Putnam & Company. London, England

1962

Uncle Dog: The Poet at 9

I did not want to be old Mr.
Garbage man, but uncle dog
who rode sitting beside him.

Uncle dog had always looked
to me to be truck-strong
wise-eyed, a cur-like Ford

Of a dog. I did not want
to be Mr. Garbage man because
all he had was cans to do.

Uncle dog sat there me-beside-him
emptying nothing. Barely even
looking from garbage side to side:

Like rich people in the backseats
of chauffeur-cars, only shaggy
in an unwagging tall-scrawny way.

Uncle dog belonged any just where
he sat, but old Mr. Garbage man
had to stop at every single can.

I thought. I did not want to be Mr.
Everybody calls them that first.
A dog is said, *Dog!* Or by name.

I would rather be called Rover
than Mr. And sit like a tough
smart mongrel beside a garbage man.

Uncle dog always went to places
unconcerned, without no hurry.
Independent like some leashless

Toot. Honorable among scavenger
can-picking dogs. And with a bitch
at every other can. And meat:

His for the barking. Oh, I wanted
to be uncle dog—sharp, high fox-
eared, cur-Ford truck-faced

With his pick of the bones.
A doing, truckman's dog
and not a simple child-dog

Nor friend to man, but an uncle
traveling, and to himself—
and a bitch at every second can.

The Kite

I still heard Auntie Blue
after she did not want to come down
again. She was skypaper, way up
too high to pull down. The wind
liked her a lot, and she was lots of noise
and sky on the end of the string.
And the string jumped hard all of a sudden,
and the sky never even breathed,
but was like it always was, slow and close
far-away blue, like poor dead Uncle Blue.

Auntie Blue was gone, and I could not
think of her face. And the string fell down
slowly for a long time. I was afraid to pull it
down. Auntie Blue was in the sky,
just like God. It was not my birthday
anymore, and everybody knew, and dug
a hole, and put a stone on it
next to Uncle Blue's stone, and he died
before I was even born. And it was too bad
it was so hard to pull her down; and flowers.

What it Was

What it was, was this: the stars
had died for the night,
and shone;
and God, God also shone,
up, straight up, at the very
top of the sky.

The street
was one of the better suburbs
of the night, and was a leaf,
or the color of one in the
moonlit dark.

She, my mother,
went to the window. It was
as late as night could be
to her.
She looked at the wind,
still, the wind,
…never having blown.

And in the morning, now, of sleep
the stars, the moon and God
began
once more, away,
into the sky.

—And she, my mother, slept…
in her window, in her sky.

A Walk in the Scenery

It is there. And we are there. In it.
Walking in it, talking, holding hands.
The nickel postcard—the glossy trees;
the waterfalls, the unsuspecting
deer. A scene shot from a car window:
a slowly moving car, with many
windows, and a good camera.
And we are walking in it. We tell
ourselves, quietly, perhaps screaming,
...quietly, "We are walking in it."
And our voices sound, somehow, as if
we were behind windows, or within.
We embrace, and are in love. The deer
we are watching, at the same time
(through cameras, binoculars, eyes...)
so perfectly wild, and concerned
—with the scene they are, their glossy fate
silence, Nature, their rotogravure pose—
that they remain, not watching; rather,
staring away from us, into the
earnest, green and inoffensive trees.

Dodo

The dodo is two feet high, and laughs.
A parrot, swan-sized, pig-, scale-legged
bird. Neither parrot, nor pig—nor swan.
Its beak is the beak of a parrot,
a bare-cheeked, wholly beaked and speechless
parrot. A bird incapable of
anything—but laughter. And silence:
a silence that is laughter—and fact.
And a denial of fact (and bird).
It is a sort of turkey, only
not a turkey; not anything. —Not
able to sing, not able to dance
not able to fly...
—The Dutch called it the 'nauseous bird,'
Walguögel, 'the uncookable.'
Its existence (extinct as it is)
is from the Portuguese: *Duodo*, 'dumb,'
'stupid,' 'silly.' And the story of its
having been eaten on Rodrigues
Island by hogs, certain sailors & monkeys:
Didus ineptus. A bird that aided
its own digestion, of seeds and leaves,
by swallowing large stones. It has been called,
though with birds (extinct or otherwise)
crosses are a lie, a cross between
a turkey and a pigeon. The first,
it is claimed, won out; and, having won,
took flight from flight (its wings but tails, gray
yellow tufted white). And for reasons
as yet unknown.

Its beak is laughter
and shines, in indifference—and size.
It has the meaning, for some, of wings:
wings that have become a face: embodied
in a beak... and half the dodo's head...
It laughs—silence, its mind, extends from its ears:
its laugh, from wings, like wrists, to bill, to ears.

Hello Poem

Hello wife, hello world, hello God,
I love you. Hello certain monsters,
ghosts, office buildings, I love you. Dog,
dog-dogs, cat, cat-cats, I love you.
Hello Things-In-Themselves, Things Not Quite
In Themselves (but trying), I love you.
River-rivers, flower-flowers, clouds
and sky;
the Trolley Museum in Maine
(with real trolleys); airplanes taking
off; airplanes not taking off; airplanes
landing,

I love you.

The IRT,
BMT; the London subway
(yes, yes, pedants, the Underground)
system; the Moscow subway system,
all subway systems except the
Chicago subway system. Ah yes,
I love you, the Chicago El-
evated. Sexual intercourse,
hello, hello.

Love, I love you; Death,
I love you;
and some other things, as well,
I love you. Like what? Walt Whitman,
Wagner, Henry Miller;
a really
extraordinary, one-legged
Tijuana whore; I love you, loved
you.
The *Reader's Digest* (their splendid,
monthly vocabulary tests), *Life*

and *Look*...
handball, volleyball, tennis;
croquet, basketball, football, Sixty-
nine;
draft beer for a nickel; women
who will lend you money, women
who will not;
women, pregnant women;
women who I am making pregnant;
women who I am not making pregnant.
Women. Trees, goldfish, silverfish,
coral fish, coral;
I love you, I
love you.

Kissing the Dancer
Cornell University Press, Ithaca, New York
1964

Kissing the Dancer

Song is not singing,
the snow

Dance is dancing,
my love

On my knees, with voice
I kiss her knees

And dance; my words are song,
for her

I dance; I give up my words,
learn wings instead

We fly like trees
when they fly

To the moon. There, there are
some now

The clouds opening, as you, as we
are there

Come in!

I love you, kiss your knees
with words,

Enter you, your eyes
your lips, like

Lover
Of us all,

words sweet words
learn wings instead.

By the Swimming

By the swimming
the sand was wetter
the farther down you dug; I dug:
my head and ear on top
of the sand, my hand felt water…
and the lake was blue not watching.
The water was just waiting there
in the sand, like a private lake.
And no one could kick sand
into my digging, and the water
kept going through my fingers slow
like the sand, and the sand was water too.
And then the wind was blowing everyplace,
and the sand smelled like the lake,
only wetter. It was raining then.
Everybody was making waxpaper noises,
and sandwiches, kicking sand
and running with newspapers on their heads.
Baldmen and bathing hat-ladies, and naked people.
And all the sand turned brown and stuck together
hard. And the sky was lightning, and the sun
looked down sometimes to see how dark it was
and to make sure the moon wasn't there.
And then we were running: and everybody was under
the hotdog tent eating things, spitting very mad
and waiting for the sky, and to go home.

Chicago's Waldheim Cemetery

We are in Chicago's Waldheim Cemetery.
I am walking with my father.
My nose, my eyes,
 left pink wrinkled oversize
ear
my whole face is in my armpit.

We are at the stone beneath which lies
my father's mother.
There is embedded in it a pearl-shaped portrait.
I do not know this woman.
I never saw her.
I am suddenly enraged, indignant.
I clench my fists. I would like to strike her.
My father weeps.
He is Russian. He weeps with
conviction, sincerity, enthusiasm.
I am attentive.
I stand there listening beside him.
After a while, a little bored,
but moved,
I decide myself to make the effort.
I have paid strict attention.
I have listened carefully.
Now, I too will attempt tears.
They are like song.
They are like flight.
I fail.

Scenes from a Text

*Several actual, potentially and/or
really traumatic situations are
depicted on these pages.*
—Transient Personality Reactions to Acute or Special Stress (Chapter 5).

Photo II

The house is burning. The furniture
is scattered on the lawn (tables, chairs
TV, refrigerator). Momma—
there is a small, superimposed white
arrow pointing at her—is busy
tearing out her eyes. The mute husband
(named, arrowed) stands idly by, his hands
upon his hips, eyes already out.
The smoke blankets the sky. And the scene,
apart from Momma, Poppa, the flames…
could be an auction. Friends, relatives
neighbors, all stand by, reaching, fighting
for the mirrors, TV, sunglasses;
the children, the cats and speechless dogs.

Nightgown, Wife's Gown

Where do people go when they go to sleep?
I envy them. I want to go there too.
I am outside of them, married to them.
Nightgown, wife's gown, women that you look at,
beside them—I knock on their shoulder blades
ask to be let in. It is forbidden.
But you're my wife, I say. There is no reply.
Arms around her, I caress her wings.

Sonnet for Two Voices

Of Love, my friends (after such sophistry
and praise as yours), may one presume? Well, then,
let me begin by begging Agathon:
Good sir, is not your love a love for me?
And not a love for those who disagree?
Yes, true! And what is it that Love, again,
is the love of? Speak! *It is the love again
of "Socrates."* Love then, and the Good, are me.

Explain! Is Love the love of something, or
the love of nothing? *Something!* Very true.
And Love desires the thing it loves. *Right.*
Is it, then, really me whom you adore?
Or is it nothing? *O Socrates, it's you!*
Then I am Good, and I am yours. *Agreed!*

Chicago

There are many underground things
in cities, things like sewers,
that run for miles, lengths
and widths, across cities,
under all. Then there are
the basements of large stores,
houses and hotels, and often
these basements run for twenty feet
and more out, around the buildings;
and coal, garbage and all kinds
of food are sent up and down into
the basements, or out, from the side-
walks and the alleys and streets,
by chutes, corrugated elevator-
stands, iron platforms, sewer tops
...round, rectangular or square.

And these metal things in the sidewalks,
streets, are always rather warm;
and in the winter, to comfort
and unbitter their sittings,
haunches and tails, and to avoid
the asphalt ice and cold, cats
and dogs, stray squirrels
and so forth, come at night
and from miles around, rest
and together partake.

And from some
distances, they and their live optic
green, brown congregations of eyes
appear as islands, still yellow
large, oval, gray or opalesque.

And no dog bites no cat, nor squirrel,
and all is quiet, idle, until the sun
comes up and chases them
out of the night, off the warmth
and good of the sewers to their parts
and tails. Then without a look
at the sun, itself, they run, trot
walking, no, no business into the snow.

All for a Day

All day I have written words.
My subject has been that: Words.
And I am wrong. And the words.
I burn
three pages of them. Words.
And the moon, moonlight, that too
I burn. A poem remains.
But in the words, in the words,
in the fire that is now words.
I eat the words that remain,
and am eaten. By nothing,
by all that I have not made.

Thousand-Year-Old Fiancée
& Other Poems
Cornell University Press, Ithaca, NY.
1965

Movies: Left to Right

The action runs left to right,
cavalry, the water-skiers—
then a 5-hour film, *The Sleeper*,
a man sleeping for five hours
(in fifteen sequences),
sleeping left to right, left to right
cavalry, a love scene, elephants.
Also the world goes left to right,
the moon and all the stars, sex too
and newspapers, catastrophe.

In bed, my wives are to my left.
I embrace them moving left to right.
I have lived my life that way,
growing older, moving eastward—
the speedometer, the bank balance
architecture, good music.
All that is most real moves left to right,
declares my friend the scenarist,
puffing on a white cigar, eating
The *Herald Tribune*, the *New Republic*.

My life is a vision, a mechanism
that runs from left to right. I have lived badly.
Water-skier, I was until recently
in the U.S. Cavalry. Following that
I played elephant to a lead by Tarzan.
Later, I appeared in a film called *The Sleeper*.
Till today, standing on the edge of things,
falling and about to fall asking, Why?
I look back. Nowhere. Meanwhile, one or more wives
goes on stilts for the mail.

Holding Hands

Always I am leaving people, missing them,
going out to them and loving them;
holding hands, doing turnabout, ah,
going to movies with them, clowning
reverential, an enthusiast—for what?
The certain good of sleeping with them,
holding them, climbing into their bellies.
I am present in them, approving their skins,
most foolish hopes, warmest impulses
and the loss
of vanity, the presence of which—
and all is lost.

Huge stars are falling,
great owls circle above us. We sit here
in wonderment—

Is there anyone
anyone anyone has not been with?
The truth is, nothing else matters.
You are, I am, he is. The world will please
come to order. Be seated. Hold hands.
No it won't. No it won't. Don't be scared.
Cover up my love, we will all of us
never not be in you, my love love's there first.

Thousand-Year-Old Fiancée

We are alone, Death's thousand-year-old fiancée
and I. The thing suggests itself to me.
I step onto the front parts of her feet,
and stand like that facing her saying nothing.
In moments I lose twenty pounds and sweat. My nose
bleeds.
It occurs to me I may never before
have acted out of instinct. We do not embrace.
She is in her middle sixties, with varicose veins,
whitish hair and buttocks as large as Russia.
Things come off of her in waves, merriment,
exuberance, benevolent body lice,
hundred-year-old blackheads. I kiss her hives.
I lick her nose that shows she drinks bottles
and bottles of vodka every day.
I am standing there in my Jewish hair
facing her with my life. Knock, knock.
It is Death in spats and a blue business suit.
I stand there in my Jewish hair facing him.
He is very still, grinning, grayish, bemused.
Pretty soon I begin to scream. All night I scream.

Yeah. After a while I go under and kiss
her ass. It takes a bit. Fathers and sons,
I am up to my knees in the moon.
Kiss this ghost she says of a certain light.
I plunge my tongue into it to the ears. Madam,
I say, astounded, choking, feverish,
I have not as yet had you. Have me, she says.
Under my foreskin there is a star, whole
constellations. Goddammit, I am not
speaking to you here of sex! Kiss me here,
she says. Kiss me there. Stars, ghosts and sons,
winged,
we are all of us winged—
the one thing
there is of us. Death, you old lecher,

I affirm you, I confront you with my balls.
I revere dead fish and sunken submarines,
the little red schoolhouse and the American way.
Let us in fact join hands with the universe.
Death, I have news for you. I climb into
your young fiancée eleven times a night.
There are signs that she is pregnant.
Death, there is nothing I will not love.

People Coming Out of People

Rings coming out of rings,
four and then eight—
you reach for one, the man says,
and you have two. That is the way
rings give birth to rings. Once speaking of cups
he cried, Each is within the other,
each is linked to each. All that he did
bore witness to this. "You are pop art,"
said his woman. Marriage is like that.
What is virtue? Reach for one
and you have two. Weariness,
that is also a truth. All conditions
are truths. Claim only those
you've a mind to. All things, all truths are gifts.
The man who dreamt of playing magician
reaching for goblets, chalices, cups
one and then within it its mate,
or linked by the handles, by rims,
like women within women
the metaphysics of sex.
That too is a question—
the man reaching,
all that he wants, doubles.
That is the way rings give birth to rings
and that is what if not a truth? (again)
cups within cups, people within people
out of love, out of need, out of want.

Five Iowa Poems
Iowa City, Iowa
1975

Iowa City, Iowa

Some years the ground pulls harder.

He mounts his tractor.
There are creatures in trees
whose names I do not know.
There are others in procession before us.
Pigs the size of buffalo. Cattle
the tails and markings of horses.
Iowa. What am I doing in Iowa?
Ann lies in the sun. Dozing. Depressed.
Stripping, rising on my hind legs,
hairy, cloven-footed,
Centaur, I declare myself: Centaur.
Then chicken. Then horse. Bull. Then pig.
She too: Centaur. Then chicken. Horse. Bull. Then pig.
Let us plant our dreams.
Write them down and plant them.
Plant sugar cubes.
Make love.
Then dig it up, turn it over
and plant the ground,
that ground we made love on.
What will grow there?
Rhubarb.
A peach tree.
The ground holds me as I make love to it.
How is it birds no longer fly?
Horses only. The entire state of Iowa.
What about deities,
these deities that eat your brains?
And why anyway should I mind that?
I am busy planting my brains.
I will harvest them remind me please before leaving.
The time has come.
O look Centaur Snowing   Your eyes
your eyes
they touch me.
I have been asleep.

Does it hurt?

Iowa

What a strange happiness.
Sixty poets have gone off drunken, weeping into the hills,
I among them.
There is no one of us who is not a fool.
What is to be found there?
What is the point in this?
Someone scrawls six lines and says them.
What a strange happiness.

Iowa Writers' Workshop—1958

For Paul Engle

Seated, against the room, against the walls
legs extended, or under chairs
iambs, trochees & knees...
we surrender, each of us, to the sheets
at hand. The author swallows his voice. Still

"Page two." Page one is saved for the last.
"The poet has here been impressed
by the relationship
between blue birds and black. In the octet
we note the crow. And its iambic death."

"On page three, *The Poet Upon His Wife*,
(by his wife) we note the symbols
for the poet: the bird
in flight, the collapsing crow, the blue bird...
Note too the resemblance between sonnets."

We vote and stare at one another's crow.
Ours is an age of light. Our crows
reflect the age, Eisenhower-Nixon
colored stripes, rainbow-solids, blacks & whites.
Ruffling their wings, Mezey, Coulette, Levine
refuse to vote.

"Page four, *Apologies to William S.*
apologies, our third sonnet..."
And those who teach, who write
and teach, the man at hand, apologize
for themselves, and themselves at hand.

"Poets buy their socks at Brooks & Warren,
like DuPont, like Edsel, like Ike."
Anecdotes, whispers, cliques
whispering, then aloud into prominence.
Brooks & Warren, DuPont, Edsel & Ike.

Order is resumed. *"We have been here, now*
forever. From the beginning
of verse." One has written
nothing, and it is inconceivable
that one would, or will ever write again.

A class has ended. They pass by, gazing
in. The poets gaze out, and grin.
They gaze out, and through the
electric voice, the ruffled sonnet sheets
that stare against the faces staring in.

"Page one." Walled-in glances at the author.
And then the author disappears,
the poem anonymous.
Voice. Voices. There are voices about it:
anonymous. The self. A sonnet's self…

The room is filled with it. It is a bird.
It sits beside us and extends
its wings. Mezey hits it with his elbow.
The bird shrieks and sprawls
upon the floor. We surrender

We surrender to its death. The poem breathes,
becomes its author and departs.
We all depart. And watch
the green walls take our seats. Apologies.
Brooks & Warren. DuPont. Edsel & Ford.

Impossible Hurricane Loss-of-Name Poem

The fields planted.
Tractors   Wooden clothespins rising.
Parched. Brown. Plows and houses. Rising.
Rainbow. It ends or begins or starts.
Is it walking or is it skipping?
It rides above the fence.
If I dig a hole will I find a poem?
A pot of unicorns?
A herd of leprechauns?
I ask. The rainbow has already moved.
Seven miles in the soft light.
A field filled with cows.
The hurricane approaches.
There are funnels filled with butterflies.
Dust that is the rain.
Thunder. Trees. The grass.
The wind walking.
Phosphorous. The rain.
The noiseless. Wind. Explodes.
I am lying in the sun only there is none.
I am being blown away   only
the moon rises   which
is the sun? Evening. There is none.
Red. Parched brown. Plows and houses.
Hurricane. Hurricane.
My name has been blown away.
O name poor name,
will the rain care for you as I have cared for you?
Will the wind devour you,
knock your head against a tree?
Already I have forgotten.
Can a young man named…
live happily in a hurricane?

Will his house and woman and poems blow away?
Once they have blown away. Twice. Already.
That the house and the woman and the unnamed man
have their tongues in one another's mouths,
can they go on like that?
Funnel, stars, butterfly,
wind. The noiseless
Yes, they can.

Movies: Left to Right
Soft Press, Victoria, B.C.
1983

Mr. Amnesia

Even an amnesiac remembers some things
better than others.
In one past life I was a subway conductor
for the Chicago subway system.

In another I was—Gosh, I forgot!
Anyway, some years ago, I was run over
by a sports car. Ever since that time

I find I cannot go more than a few days
without leaving my body at least briefly
and then coming back to it. Again and again.

I can't seem to stay in Chicago or in any city,
for that matter, and in one body,
for very long.

I once wrote a forty-nine-line poem
made up entirely of first lines, forty-nine beginnings.
Forty-nine Beginnings it was called.

I once met a young mother who had gone fishing
with her two children. Coming up from the bottom
of Lake Michigan, I got tangled up in their lines

And they pulled me out and saved my life.
The woman was my wife and the children were
my children.
"Making love, it's always as if it were happening

"for the first time," I said after ten years of marriage.
"When a woman chooses an amnesiac as her husband,
she has to expect things like that," she laughed.

"Still, there's a lot to be said
for ten years of foreplay."
An Instructor in Modern Poetry, I once lectured

For four weeks as if each class was the first class
of a new year. When the genial Chairman,
manifesting polite alarm,

Visited my classes, the occasion of his being there
gave me the opportunity to teach
as if those classes, too, were new classes.

Promoted, given a raise, a bonus and a new two-year
contract,
even I was confused. Each class I taught became one
in an infinite series of semesters, each semester

Lasting no more than fifty minutes.
I don't know about you, but I hardly unpack
and get ready for this lifetime and it's time

To move on to the next. I've been reincarnated
three times,
and am forty-nine years old and I don't even know
my own name.
History is just one of those things

You learn to live without. I live in a city
the entire population of which is made up of amnesiacs
so for the first time in three lifetimes I feel at home.

Half a Life's History

Aya Press Poetry Series: No. 4, Toronto, Ont.

1983

Half a Life's History

(Excerpted from The Jurassic Shales, A Novel,
Coach House Press, Toronto, 1983)
Scenario: *An amnesiac wakes one morning
in London, England, in bed with two women. In the
process of recovering his memory, he goes back in
time 160 million years to the Jurassic geological
period to find his true original parents, the first
of the flying dinosaurs. The narrator is himself
a flying dinosaur, and* The Jurassic Shales *ends
with his being united with his father and mother.*

Here I am writing to you
half a life's history
"A horse which throws the dreamer to the ground."
I am homesick and America has had a nervous breakdown.
I am taking shaman lessons and studying Karate.
My greatest complaint (you've offered to help) is amnesia.
Do you believe in transmigration of the soul? Yes, I do too.
But what if it can happen not only when one dies, but
several times in an afternoon?
And I'm sure it's not properly amnesia I am speaking of.
I go out of my body, I come back in.
I say amnesia because sometimes when this happens
I forget just who I am.
I've been doing this, I believe, with some regularity
for a quarter of a million years. I'm doing it more
and more frequently now because I'm unhappy.
Even the light depresses me. That is, the light
on Oxford Street, 6 PM on a Sunday. The light
in Bloom's. The light in Wimpy's. I haven't seen
light like this since the Middle Ages of the Animals.

We drink, we smoke, we go to parties. Friday night
we went to the dullest party in 3,000 years
in Bayswater off the Moscow Road.

I thought the whole time of algae, worms,
primitive brachiopods, mollusks, crustaceans,
I thought of my mother and those birds with the hollow
bones.
I am in the library at Swiss Cottage
eating chocolates in the children's room
What am I reading? Probably I have gone mad.
I am reading up on the eohippus, the first true
archaic horse.
I identify. Those horses were no larger than dogs.
I'm a dog and interested in horses
that were once my own size.
Why? I don't know why. Yes, I do. It's because
I feel I was once (also) a wooly rhinoceros.
That I am at this moment a wooly rhinoceros.
Anyway, I am no longer incapacitated by my erotic
fantasies.
I am devoting my whole attention to insects, geology, etc.
Each morning I have friends come in to read me my
biography and my passport.
Then I know who I am. Then I can pay attention
to what needs to be done.

Who are these people anyway? They think they speak English,
but I don't understand a word they say.
My only reason for coming was to learn Karate with Kanazawa,
who has left for Germany.
Oh, I've just gone out of my body and now I'm back.
What is happening in America where, I am convinced,
in my previous existence, I was a Confederate
        soldier killed in action, 186-?
Well, it doesn't matter. I'll find out soon enough and probably
        know anyway if I'd only think about it.

Scarf Gobble Wallow Inventory

How hungry and for what are the people this season
predicting the end of the end of the end of
I've only just come home after having been away
The world sends its greetings and the greetings
send greetings
Hello goodbye, hello goodbye
There are greetings and gifts everywhere
Children screaming and feeling slighted
The next minute we're walking along canals
on the planet Mars
Twenty minutes later we are earthworms in black
leather jackets, our pockets filled
with hamburgers,
Voyage to the moon.
All I am really hungry for is everything
The ability to hibernate and a red suitcase going off
everywhere
Every cell in your body and every cell in my body is
hungry and each has its own stomach
Are your cells eating my cells? Whose cell is the
universe, and what is it sick with, if anything?
Is the universe a womb or a mouth?
And what is hunger, really?
And is the end of the world to be understood in terms of
hunger or gifts, or the tops of peoples' heads
coming off?
The most complex dream I've ever dreamed I dreamed
in London.
It involved in its entirety taking one bite of an orange.

*   *   *

"What do you want to be when you grow up?" she says.
I'm nearly sixty.
I want to be hungry as I am now and a pediatrician.
The truth is I'm 45 and hungrier than I was when I was
20 and a sailor.
I'm hungry for ice cream made with ice cream and not
chemicals or artificial spoons.
I've never been so hungry in my life.
I want one more bacon-lettuce-and-tomato
sandwich,
to make love and kiss everyone I know goodbye.
Tomorrow at half past four we will all four-and-a-half
billion of us walk slowly into orbit.
If only one can do this breathing normally, and not trip
on one's breath or have stomach cramps or clammy
hands or hysterical needs or a coughing fit or the wish
to trample or stomp someone, but stepping peacefully
There is ALL the time in the world
There is ALL THE TIME IN THE WORLD
There is all the time in the world.

Statement of Poetics, or
"Goodbye To Myself"

I wrote for myself for people.
I've changed,
I've changed since I began writing
I write for myself. I believe
more than ever in music, in the sound,
however gotten, of music
in people's poetry. Rhyme
more than ever. Talk
people talking, getting that
into one's poetry that
is my poetics. Love
hate lies laughing stealings
self-confession, self-destruction.
No one has to read them. No one
has to publish them.
I am more
and more for unpublished poetry.
That is why I have a pseudonym, that
is why I now publish poetry.
To hell with the Business
of Anthologies. To hell with Anthologies.

One way and another I have written angry
for twenty years. Now I want music and
the sounds of people.
I want poems that use the word *heart* and
self-confession and incorrect
grammar and the soils and stains of Neruda
and Lorca and Kabir and Williams and
Whitman and Yeats.

Forty-four years old. Stand on my head
ten minutes daily morning
breakfast, supper.
Writing less and less.
Evaporating into the air
feet first. I won't
ever die. I'll simply
stand on my head
and disappear into the
air just like that.

I don't believe in imagination. The prairies
as a landscape are imagination. England is,
as a landscape, a failure of imagination.
Kenya is imagination, India
is reaching even further
than that. And that is why I will
go to India, which I will in seven
days time. So this
is a time capsule
in case anyone is
interested and in case
I never come back.

Goodbye for
now, goodbye
goodbye goodbye
to myself,
goodbye goodbye
for now
goodbye myself,
goodbye for
now goodbye.

(1977)

Poet Santa Cruz

Jazz Press, Santa Cruz, CA
1985

Ode to Santa Cruz

For Sandy Lydon

You want a sunrise? asks the poet,
I'll give you a sunrise. Eggplant cirrus clouds,
pinky smoky blue and gray,
pink, moss pink, pink nether flower
sunrise, sunrise
yellow white silicon chip
foghorn, windchime, no-color haze.

Sunrise sunrise
O City of Mystical Arts and Live Soup,
Antique bathhouse, casino
Riva Fish House,

A busload of German tourists
applauding *(applaudieren!)*
the sunrise.
clam chowder, O scrubbed blue light
melon balls and watermelon shooters,
arcade, pink neon, roller coaster heart-shaped mirror.

KA-BOOM! House begins to dance,
land moves in waves three and four feet high,
weight machines swaying, mirrors rattling,
a sidewalk of broken glass,
a street filled with jewels.
Loma Prieta, The Earthquake of the Dark Hill,
place, this place, always coming back from a disaster.
Natural beauty and unnatural events,
jazz, blues, canoes, tattoos,
I bow and give thanks to the muse,
Santa Cruz, O Santa Cruz!

Castroville, California
—A Coffee Shop Cum Art Gallery

Sonnet

O thistle-like artichoke in the place
of glory. Green peppers: four lushly framed nudes
staring down on us with a kind of greasy grace.
Purple and green eggplants like immodest prudes.

And apples of heroic size, left to right
like paintings of smugly pompous ancestors.
Broccoli plus pale mushrooms in the moonlight,
whitely bulbous omniscient lecturers

On the care and curatorship of fruit
and vegetables, which play more a part
in our lives than the sad-eyed, ruling dupes
who clutter up our walls displacing fruits.

I never did before, but now I will:
I sing, dear friends, of brave plain Castroville.

LI PO

c. 700-760 A.D.
—after Robert Payne's *The White Pony*

Tall, powerfully built with a loud screeching voice
and bright, hungry tigerish eyes, his black hair
flowing over his shoulders.
The high heavenly priest of the white lake
with murderers and thieves for ancestors.
Musician, swordsman and connoisseur of fine wines,
a drunk, a murderer—
Mr. Fairyland, Mr. Landscape of an
impossible flowering.
He was called a god in exile, the great phoenix
whose wings obscure the sun.
"I am strong enough," boasted this poet, "to meet
ten thousand men."

Li Po who, at death, was summoned by angelic hosts,
who rode off on the backs of dolphins
and, led by the two children of immortality,
entered the celestial palace in triumph.

The Emperor

A villanelle from:
  The Way And Its Power

The world as seen in vision has no name;
call it the Sameness or the Mystery
or rather the "Darker than any Mystery."

Fan Li who, offered half a kingdom,
stepped into a light boat and was heard from
no more. The world as seen in vision has no name.

An empty vessel that one draws from
without its ever needing to be filled. The name-
less, the darker than any Mystery.

Can you love people, rule the land,
yet remain unknown? Play always the female part?
The world as seen in vision has no name.

Rear them, feed them, but do not lay claim.
He who in dealing with the empire,
darker than any mystery,

Regards his high rank as though it were
his body, is the best person to be entrusted with rule.
The world as seen in vision has no name;
call it the Darker than any Mystery.

Four Incarnations
Coffee House Press, Minneapolis, MN
1991

Foreword:

Four Incarnations

Born on the Jewish North Side of Chicago, *bar mitzvahed*, sailor, amnesiac, university professor (Cornell, Iowa, Connecticut College), newspaper editor, food reviewer, father of five children, husband to four wives, my writing career has been described by critic Virginia Lee as a "long and winding road."

1. Switchblade Poetry: Chicago Style

I began writing poetry in Chicago at age 15, when I was named corresponding secretary for a gang of young punks and hoodlums called the Semcoes. A Social Athletic Club, we met at various locations two Thursdays a month. My job was to write postcards to inform my brother thugs—who carried switchblade knives and stole cars for fun and profit—as to when, where and why we were meeting.

Rhyming couplets seemed the appropriate form to notify characters like light-fingered Foxman, cross-eyed Harris, and Irving "Koko," of upcoming meetings. My switchblade juvenilia:

The Semcoes meet next Thursday night
at Speedway
Koko's. Five bucks dues, Foxman, or fight.

Koko, a young boxer. His father owned Chicago's Speedway Wrecking Company, basement filled with punching bags and pinball machines. Koko and the others joked about my affliction—the writing of poetry—but were so astonished that they criticized me mainly for my inability to spell.

2. Sailor Librarian: San Diego

At 17, I graduated from high school, gave up my job
as soda jerk and joined the Navy. The Korean War
was underway; my mother had died, and Chicago seemed
an oppressive place to be.

My thanks to the U.S. Navy. They taught me how
to type (60 words a minute), organize an office, and
serve as a librarian. In 1952 I served in Korea aboard a
300-foot long, flat-bottomed Landing Ship Tank (LST).
A Yeoman 3rd Class, I became overseer of 1200
paperback books, a sturdy upright typewriter, and a
couple of filing cabinets.

The best thing about duty on an LST is the ship's
speed: 8-10 knots. It takes approximately one month
for an LST to sail between San Diego and Pusan, Korea.
In that month I read Melville's MOBY DICK,
Whitman's LEAVES OF GRASS, Thoreau's WALDEN,
Isak Dinesen's WINTER'S TALES, the King James Version
of the Bible, Shakespeare's HAMLET, KING LEAR, and a
biography of Abraham Lincoln.

While at sea, I began writing poetry as if poems,
to paraphrase Thoreau, were secret letters from
some distant land.

I sent one poem to a girl named Lorelei with whom
I was in love. Lorelei had a job at the Dairy Queen.
Shortly before enlisting in the Navy, I spent $15. of
my soda jerk money taking her up in a single engine,
sight-seeing airplane so we could kiss and—at the
same time—get a good look at Chicago from the air.
Beautiful Loreli never responded to my poem. Years
later, at the University of Iowa Writers' Workshop,
I learned that much of what I had been writing (love
poems inspired by a combination of lust and
loneliness) belonged, loosely speaking, to a
tradition—the venerable tradition of unrequited love.

3. Mr. Amnesia: Cambridge

In 1962, after ten years of writing poetry, my book,
UNCLE DOG & OTHER POEMS, was published by Putnam
in England. That was followed by two books from
Cornell University Press, KISSING THE DANCER and
THOUSAND-YEAR-OLD FIANCÉE. Then in 1966, I was
invited to do 14 poetry readings in a two-week
stretch at places like Dartmouth, Amherst, and the
University of Connecticut.

The day before I was scheduled to embark on the
reading series, I was hit by a speeding MG in
Cambridge, Massachusetts.

I lost my memory for a period of about 24 hours.
Just as I saw the world fresh while cruising to a
war zone, so I now caught a glimpse of what a city
like Cambridge can look like when one's inner slate,
so to speak, is wiped clean.

4. Santa Claus: Santa Cruz

In December, 1985, recently returned to the U.S.
after some years in Canada, a free lance writer
in search of a story, I sought and found
employment as a Rent-a-Santa Claus. Imagine walking
into the local Community Center and suddenly, at the
sight of 400 children, feeling transformed from
one's skinny, sad-eyed self, into an elf—having to
chant the prescribed syllables, "Ho, Ho, Ho."

What is poetry? For me, it's the restrained music
of a switchblade knife. It's an amphibious warship
magically transformed into a basketball court, and
then transformed again into a movie theater showing
a film about the life of Joan of Arc. It is the
vision of an amnesiac, bleeding from a head injury,
witnessing the play of sunlight on a redbrick wall.

Poetry comes to a bearded Jewish wanderer, pulling
on a pair of high rubber boots with white fur, and a
set of musical sleigh bells, over blue, fleece-lined
sweat pants. It comes to the father of five
children bearing gifts for 400 and, choked up,
unable to speak, alternately laughing and sobbing
the three traditional syllables—Ho, Ho, Ho—hearing
at the same time, in his heart, the more plaintive,
tragic—*Oi vay, Oi vay, Oi vay.*

Clancy The Dog

For Claire

He is so ugly he is a psalm to ugliness,
this extra-terrestrial, short-haired
midget sea lion,
snorts, farts, grunts, turns somersaults
on his mistress' bed.

She calls him an imperfect Boston terrier,
part gnome, part elf,
half something and half something else,
180,000,000-year-old Clancy
with his yellowy-white, pin-pointy teeth
and red, misshapen pre-historic gums.

Clancy has no tail at all and doesn't bark.
He squeaks like a monkey,
flies through the air,
lands at six every morning
on his mistress' head,
begging to be fed and wrapped not in a robe
but a spread.

Tree frog, wart hog, ground hog,
"Clancy, Clancy," she calls for him
in the early morning fog,
and he appears, anything, anything,
part anything, but a dog.

Scarlet the Parrot

Scarlet perches on the office windowsill
shrieking, hollering, barking

Like a dog. She knocks her mottled beak
against the warehouse window

And tries to open
the metal hook and eye latch.

There are parrot droppings
on the telephone and Scarlet has eaten

Part of the plastic receiver.
The parrot slides like a red fireman

With yellow and blue feathers
up and down the cord,
holding on

With her beak, maneuvering gracefully
with her claws.
When I approach she calls, "Hello, hello…"

Walks up my trouser leg holding on
with her macaw's beak. I feed the bird

Oranges and pears, almonds
and sunflower seeds.

I swivel my head round and round
in imitation of her neck movements.

"What's happening?" she asks,
and again, "What's happening?"

"Hello, cookie. Yoo-hoo…
Can you talk, can you talk?" she asks

Chewing for several minutes,
finally swallowing
a leather button

Off my green corduroy jacket, threatening,
ready to tear my ear off,

Biting if I place my finger
in her mouth. Her tongue is black

And her beady eyes piercing like an eagle's.
She wants a response, tests my reactions.

Tenderly the parrot walks up my corduroy jacket,
sensually restraining her claws. I'm aroused.

When a dog barks, she barks too: *Rrf, rrf.*
Casually, a relaxed but authentic

Imitation. "Hello, darling," she breathes,
looking me in the eye knowing I know

If it pleases her she might bite my ear off.
"Yoo-hoo, yoo-hoo, now you say something," she says.

Alfa the Dog

It isn't enough that when I go off for three weeks to an
artists' colony and phone home, the first thing my wife
tells me is there's a new addition to the family, a seven-
month-old poodle named Alfa and that Alfa has papers,
an honest-to-God pedigree that includes not only aristo-
cratic ancestors, but recent appearances in "The New York
Review of Books" and a novel published by Houghton-
Mifflin. And when I am somewhat less than ecstatic,
my wife asks me to at least say a few words to the new
addition, and puts on Alfa the dog. "Speak, Alfa, speak,"
I hear her say. And Alfa who is, by all accounts, loyal
and obedient, a noted storyteller, intelligent and amusing
as Oscar Wilde, refuses to speak, to bark, or make some
witty remark like, "What's the weather like in Saratoga?"
All I hear is Alfa's low doggy breathing and the tinkle
of the elegant silver bell on her collar.

My wife comes back on and says, "I have an idea. You
bark into the phone. Alfa will answer back."

Well, it's only costing a dollar ninety-five a minute and
good-natured soul that I am, devoted to my wife, guilty
at running off for three weeks, I put myself into it, throw
back my head and howl, barking, yowling, yipping like a
real dog—a dog without papers, a dog with fleas, a dog
like one of those mutts I knew growing up in Chicago,
and this happening, of course, on the public pay phone
at Yaddo, the "artists' heaven," what the *New York Times*
calls the Harvard of Artists' Colonies.

Looking up, sure enough, I see one of America's more
distinguished composers with his mouth open, his pipe
falling to the floor, waiting in line, no doubt, to speak
to his wife and children and his cats and dogs.

"Well, darling," I say, "we've been talking for twenty-five minutes. This is going to cost a fortune."

At that moment, Alfa decides she wants to make her presence known to all concerned, and she begins barking into the phone, answering me in kind, responding yip for yip, and yap for yap, lest there be any doubt in anyone's mind as to who it is I have been speaking— me to Alfa the dog, Alfa the dog to me.

Three Roberts

From heart to heart
from brain to brain
from Robert to Robert

Robert Zend phones Robert
Sward. *Ring, ring.*
"Robert, this is Robert."

"Is this Robert?" "This
is Robert, Robert." "Yes,
Robert?" I say, "This

"Is Robert, too." "Ah,
excuse me, I need
to find a match,"

Says Robert Zend putting
down the telephone
and rummaging for matches,

Granting me, a non-smoker,
the status of accessory
to his addiction.

All this occurring a few
seconds into an otherwise
scintillating conversation.

"I had a very pleasant afternoon
while reading your poems,"
Margaret Trudeau once remarked

About Zend's book, FROM ZERO TO ONE,
and I can fully understand
her saying that.

Zend translates serious things
into funny things
and funny things

Into serious things.
He also translates himself
into other people, and

Other people into himself—
and where does one of us end
and the other begin?

And where does Zend begin
and where do I zend?
I mean, end?

And what about Robert Priest?
Is he a visible man,
an invisible man?

Or the man who broke out of the Letter X?
Is he a spaceman in disguise?
A blue pyramid? A golden trumpet?

A chocolate lawnmower?
An inexhaustible flower?
Or a reader who escaped

From some interstellar library?
Rock Musician in residence
at the University of the Moon?

And meanwhile Robert Zend
looks into his mirror
and sees not Zend

But Chicago-born Uncle Dog;
Half a Life's History;
Mr. Amnesia; Mr. Movies: Left To Right;

Mr. Transmigration of the Soul;
the poet as wanderer;
a forty-nine-year-old human violin...

Robert Zend the Nomad
gazing in like an acrobat
at the window in the sky.

Ring, ring. "Robert, this
is Robert." "Is this Robert?"
"This is Robert, Robert."

"Yes, Robert," I say speaking
to my friend Robert One,
"This is Robert Two."

Roberts...
Robertness...
Three Knights of a Robert hood.

Basketball's The American Game Because It's Hysterical

"Basketball's the American game because it's hysterical,"
says Lorrie Goldensohn as the players and coaches come
off the bench and the crowd is on its feet yelling and
the Knicks are ahead 97-95 with just over three minutes
to go in the fourth quarter and Perry hits from the side
and Lorrie's husband, Barry, comes downstairs with a
bottle of scotch and a guide to English verse.

"Unless there is
a new mind, there cannot be a new line," he reads
refilling our glasses.
"Without invention the line
will never again take on its ancient
divisions…"

All evening we have been watching the New York Knicks
battling the Boston Celtics and having a running
argument about free verse, traditional rhyming poetry,
syllabic verse ("what's the point in counting for
counting's sake?"), the critic Hugh Kenner, John
Hollander's *Rhyme's Reason*, the variable foot and
the American idiom.

"In and out by Williams," says the announcer, "he's got
a nose for the basket." The crowd is on its feet
again, roaring.

"We know nothing and can know nothing
but the dance, to dance to a measure
contrapuntally,
Satyrically, the tragic foot," Barry continues.

The Celtics race down the court. "Talk about the
green wave coming at you." Bird hits and the Celtics
even the score.

"Basketball's the American game because it's like the
variable foot," says Lorrie, "it's up in the air
all the time. It's quick and the floor is continually
moving and there's this short back and forth factor."

"What I like best about the game," I say, "is shutting
my eyes and tuning out the announcer and hearing
Barry read and arguing about poetry and drinking
and listening all the while to the music of
seven-foot black herons in gym shoes, ten giant
gazelles, the stirring squeak of twenty over-size
sneakers on the varnished floor, a floor which
has been carefully and ingeniously miked in advance
for sound."

On My Way to the Korean War...

For President Dwight Eisenhower

On my way to the Korean War,
I never got there.
One summer afternoon in 1952,
I stood instead in the bow
of the Attack Transport *Menard*,
with an invading force
of 2,000 battle-ready Marines,
watching the sun go down.
Whales and porpoises,
flying fish and things jumping
out of the water.
Phosphoresence—
Honolulu behind us,
Inchon, Korea, and the war ahead.

Crew cut, 18-year-old librarian,
Yeoman 3rd Class, editor
of the ship's newspaper,
I wrote critically if unoriginally
of our Commander-in-Chief,
Mr. President,
and how perplexing it was that he
would launch a nuclear-powered submarine
while invoking the Lord,
Crocodile Earth shaker,
Shiva J. Thunderclap,
choosing the occasion to sing
the now famous *Song of the Armaments*,
the one with the line "weapons for peace":

O weapons for peace,
O weapons for peace,
awh want, awh want
more weapons for peace!

At sundown, a half dozen sailors
converged on the bow of the ship
where, composed and silent,
we'd maintain our vigil
until the sun had set.

Careful to avoid being conspicuous,
no flapping or flailing of the arms,
no running, horizontal take-offs,
one man, then another, stepped out into space,
headed across the water,
moving along as if on threads.
After a while, I did the same:
left my body just as they left theirs.

In-breathe, out-breathe, and leave,
in-breathe, out-breathe, and leave.
Leave your body, leave your body,
leave your body, leave your body,

we sang as we went out
to where the light went,
and whatever held us to that ship
and its 2,000 battle-ready troops, let go.
So it was, dear friends, I learned to fly.
And so in time must you
and so will the warships,
and the earth itself,
and the sky,
for as the prophet says, the day cometh
when there will be no earth left to leave.

O me, O my,
O me, O my,
goodbye earth, goodbye sky.
Goodbye, goodbye.

1950s / 1960s

Pre-med
thinking he's
got to learn about the world
all over again from
square one

Doesn't think he knows anything for sure
only the hula-hoops and Twinkies,
the blues and violets of his mind
very late at night

red and pink lipstick case
with a little mirror on one side,
hat, stockings, garter belt
and gloves

He bought a shirt in 1950 the most remarkable
feature of which is
that a snag or tear will reduce it
to nothing.

It's a shirt made of a single cell
that, when it's reduced to nothing,
a single cell remains.
The original cell of that fabric.

What he is seeking is a quilt
made up of the original cells of all the fabrics.

What the 1950s does
like a blow to the back or side of one's head
it relocates your mind

*   *   *

'Delicious' apples and the popularity of DDT

James Dean
Peter Lawford,
Elizabeth Taylor,
the Mickey Mouse Club
taken seriously

The time many people who came into their own
in the 1960s
first got laid

The Rosenberg's frying in the electric chair
McCarthy and his crony Roy Cohn
the atomic bomb already five years old

Nixon: "California politics is a can of worms"
Captain Kangaroo, Howdy Doody

*   *   *

Inhaling
The jazz was good
Death was softened, advancements made
in the salesmanship of everything

His own deepest impulses
were not to nurse or nurture
but to hang out again
at Sonny Berkowitz' Pool Hall,
wearing blue suede shoes,
Levis and navy blue shirt.
He bought a zip gun,
joined a street gang

Once, joint in hand,
exploring the intricacies
of the Chicago Drainage Canal,
he entered a sewer
and ambled deeply as he could
reflecting all the while
on his chances of surviving
the synchronized flushing
of three-and-a-half million toilets.

For the first time in 2,000 years
one went four years to a University
without hearing one true word;
going to work for Hallmark Greeting cards
or the phone company
one knew something was at hand because things
became easy.
Tin-Pan alley
people in college dormitories subscribing
to *Photoplay*
and *The Nail Polish Review*.

Five foot two, eyes of blue,
cotton candy hair
fluffy lavender
angora sweater
short white socks
with fat cuffs
one of a hundred couples
in a Champaign, Illinois
dormitory lounge.

Rock Hudson singing to Doris Day,
…beautiful girl,
your eyes, your hair
is beyond compare…
*(*PILLOW TALK*)*

"Touch me, touch me,"
guiding his hand
into her pleated wool skirt,
'petting' it was called,
one foot touching the floor at all times
ejaculating
somewhere or other
somehow or other
discreetly as possible
love in the 1950s.

He sees giant mushroom cloud
father of the H-Bomb Edward Teller

an entire island,
Eniwetok,
radioactive coral dust
a gigantic cauliflower, blue and gray
and mauve...
five million tons of TNT

Police Action Korea Harry Truman
and Dwight David Eisenhower,
each with six legs and arms
dancing to the music
of Lord Shiva and Judy Garland
doing it
on a pink velvet loveseat

some twenty-five miles into the stratosphere,
and spread a hundred miles across the sky.

Ode to Torpor

Glory be to God for the tiresome and tedious,
Glory be to God for tedium,
for no news about anything,

for newspaper strikes and power outages,
lethargy and downtime.

Postpone and delay. And again,
postpone and delay.
No place to go. No way to get there.
No reason not to stay.

Glory be to God for inaction,
for not getting things done,
for not getting anything done,

No huffin', no puffin',
just some of that slow and easy,
the woman lackadaisically on top,
the man lackadaisically on top.
Yummy, yummy, take your time,
yummy, yummy, I'll take mine.

Slow and easy,
slow and easy.
Glory be to God, O glory.

O glory be to God.

Continuous Topless Strippers

An eight-speaker sound system,
two continuous topless strippers,
Elvis Presley singing *Early Morning Rain.*

Everyone loves television.
And because the management doesn't want
to offend anyone's tastes by omitting

So important an element
in the desired sensory mix—
"The lowest common denominator

"Creates an art form," my friend
mutters into his beer—
the five-foot by seven foot color TV

Is seen on stage backing up the strippers,
the TV little more than a concentration
of bright flashing lights which,

On closer examination, turn out
to be the Six o'clock Evening News.
"Some damn half-deranged diplomat,

"Portfolio this, portfolio that,
is dithering about something or other somewhere
or other for no reason that neither you nor I

"Nor anyone else has any idea." My friend
orders another, and I order another.
The announcer, meanwhile, is selling hangover

Or headache pills and the difficulty we all have
on occasion of falling asleep or eliminating
properly or what happens when we drink too much
coffee

And that and everything else at last dissolves
the dancers achieving what appears, in fact, to be
a new breakthrough

In negotiations, winning
in the ovation that follows
their performance

Not only our freedom
but the release and freedom
of all hostages.

48 Poets Named Robert

1.

Yes, I met Robert Frost and Robert Lowell and Robert Creeley,
Robert Duncan, Robert Mezey, Robert Bly, Robert Peterson,
appeared in *A Controversy of Poets, An Anthology of Contemporary
American Poetry* edited by Robert Kelly, but not in *New Poets of
England and America* edited by Robert Pack, admire the work of
Robert Bridges, Robert Browning, Robert Burns, Bobbie Creeley,
Robert Dana, Robert Finch, Roberto Galvan, Robert Graves,
Robert Hass, Robert Herrick, Robert Hogg, Yo! Bob Holman,
Robert Huff, Robert Kroetsch, Robert Lax, Robbie McCauley,
Robert McGovern, Roberta Mandel, Robert Peters,
Robert Pinsky, Robert Southey, Robert Louis Stevenson and
Roberto Vargas, and even performed in taverns and coffee
houses in London, Ontario, and in Toronto at Major Robert's
Restaurant—near the intersection of Major and Robert Street—
with Canadian poets Robert Priest and Robert Zend, the three of us,
billed as the Three Roberts, dedicating our readings to CBC Radio's
Robert Weaver and Robert Prowse, to the critic Robert Fulford,
with half a dedication to our friend John Robert Colombo, and to
Robert Service.

2.

But as each of my four wives explained, patiently or otherwise,
over a period of four decades, "Robert, it doesn't pay. Robert,
there's no future in it. I'm not going to go on like this…" and
"Robert, doesn't it depress you to go into libraries and see all
those books by all those other writers named Robert, even
the ones not named Robert, that practically no one on earth
is going to read?" Well, yes, it's true it doesn't pay. And it's true
there's no future in it. And it does depress me that practically
no one in America reads poetry, and that is why I took a job
writing software user manuals after teaching for fourteen years.
But then, unable to let go of what I'd done, resigned in order
to go back and write more poetry. And today I think
of you all as I re-read mail from 1984, the year I left Canada.

Three letters. One from Robert Priest, the Canadian poet.
He writes of the death by drowning of Robert B.,
and the deaths also of poets not named Robert.
And Earle 'Robert' Birney, he says, who, at 75 was seen
by the editor of *New: American & Canadian Poetry*
in a Toronto rainstorm in the throes of love running up
Yonge Street bearing flowers for his 35-year-old sweetheart;
Birney who, at 79 fell out of a tree from which
he'd been trying to dislodge a kite, and who, not long after,
recovering from an injured hip, resumed cycling
on a regular basis at breakneck speed through a North
Toronto cemetery; Birney, he says, alive and in his 80s,
had visitors who read him his poems, poems that,
when Birney heard them, with impaired memory,
he enjoyed, though he was unable to understand
he was the author of those poems.

Letter #2: Nicky 'Bob' Drumbolis, proprietor
of a Toronto bookstore, writes that his rent has gone up
$700 a month, that he must give up the store, and
that he is 'earnestly clearing stock for the big move.'

And Roberto 'Robbie' Roberts, A Publisher, writes
that he has become part owner of Omega Apparel,
a business to which he now devotes all his time. He's not
doing any more poetry these days, only neckties.

3.

I drift off at my computer and dream of Robert Zend,
whose heart gave out that same year and of Robert Priest
and Robert Graves, and in the dream I see myself reading
my favorite Graves poems to Graves, and he is lucid as
my father before his heart stopped at 82, and just before I wake,
Graves tells me I am a cross between Halley's comet and Rip
Van Winkle the way I go off to England, France, Mexico,
Canada, and then, years later, return, meeting the
sons and daughters of the people, of the Roberts I once knew,
and that that is what poems are supposed to do,
and that I have been living more like a poem than a man
with his feet on the ground, and that in the time that remains
I should be living more like a man with his feet on the ground
and less like a poem.

For Gloria On Her 60th Birthday, Or Looking For Love In Merriam-Webster

"Beautiful, splendid, magnificent,
delightful, charming, appealing,"
says the dictionary.
And that's how I start… But I hear her say,
"Make it less glorious and more Gloria."

Imperious, composed, skeptical, serene,
lustrous, irreverent,
she's marked by glory, she attracts glory
"Glory," I say, "Glory, Glory."

"Is there a hallelujah in there?"
she asks, when I read her lines one and two.
"Not yet," I say, looking up from my books.
She protests, "Writing a poem isn't the same

"As really attending to me." "But it's for
your birthday," I say. Pouting,
playfully cross, "That's the price you pay
when your love's a poet."

She has chestnut-colored hair,
old fashioned Clara Bow lips,
moist brown eyes…
arms outstretched, head thrown back
she glides toward me and into her seventh decade.

Her name means "to adore,"
"to rejoice, to be jubilant,
to magnify and honor as in worship, to give or ascribe glory—"
my love, O Gloria, I do, I do.

from Family—A Miscellany

The Family is the Country of the Heart

1. Three for Love

108,000 Ways of Making Love

Her lips are full, magenta-red
in color—

Bare-chested, she wears a yellow silk
loin cloth.
I cup my right hand
under her blue chin
and bend to kiss her,
encircling her waist with my left arm.

Her back to me, she turns

Strings of pearls,
lion-claw necklaces and
rubies and gold round her neck.

Her skin is dark,
dark as the skin of the blue god.
She has thick, reddish-brown hair
and brown eyes.

She's wearing garlands
of fresh wild flowers,
gold rings on every finger,
red and golden bangles
carved like serpents round
both ankles.

 I stroke her pearly, iridescent thighs,
tenderly smacking
as she tenderly slaps and smacks me back,

Our bodies etched with scratches
of our sharp nails

…hooting and chirruping
with the brazen night birds
gazing in at us
from half-open windows
and doorways

Framed by purple, green,
red-pink twilit bougainvillea.

She presses her big toe
and also her next
to biggest toe, and the toe
next to that, and all her other toes,
high up into my crotch
as I gently guide her with my hand.

I enter her with my mouth
and she with her mouth
does the same
as I enter her from the front
and behind,
even as she lowers herself onto my body,
even as I rise to pull her
to me.
Mirrors installed in the ceilings and walls
illustrate what we dedicate ourselves to:

Making love in 108,000 ways
all at the same time.

2. Kiss Bite And Moo Softly

Muse voice is loved woman mumbling.

Going shopping with the muse
you come away buying the right things:
rare books and cashmere pullovers for him,
silk dresses, a gold and amethyst necklace for her.
Her skin
fair and fine as the yellow
lotus, eyes bright as orbs
of a fawn, well-cut with reddish
corners. Bosom hard,
full and high, neck
goodly shaped as the conch
shell. Love seed. Kama
salila, the water of life.
Swan-like gait. Note
of the Kokila-bird. Kisses
don't interrupt sentences.
Sleeping
her arms fall into the same
position
as the Statue of Liberty.

3. Jealousy

She buys a green corduroy jacket
with a velvet collar
and a label that reads
Crazy Horse

But tries it on first in the fitting room
where I pull her to me,
reaching up
under her blouse,
nuzzling her breasts,
stroking her back,
my hands jealous of my lips,
my lips jealous of my hands

I tell her of my jealousy, and she confesses
to an urge to call me on the phone
at that time of the afternoon
when I'm likely to be at home.

She becomes annoyed
at my unfaithfulness,
that instead of being there to answer the phone
I lie beside her,
stroking
exploring
our lips joined,
until at last
rolling together on the fitting room floor—

"I want to speak with you," she breathes,
"and have you all to myself,
I want to hear you call for me and moan.
Lover, oh lover," she sighs at last
"I want to call now and tell my lover,
oh, my lover, oh, my lover."

Hannah

Her third eye is strawberry jam
has a little iris in it
her eyelids
are red
she's sleepy
and the milk
has gone down
the wrong way.
I've just had breakfast
with the smallest person in the world.

Portrait of an L.A. Daughter

Take #1

Braided blonde hair
white and pink barrettes
Bette Davis gorgeous
I hug her
dreamy daughter with no make-up
silver skull and crossbones
middle
finger
ring
three or four others in each ear
rings in her navel
rings on her thumbs
gentle moonchild
"pal" she announces
to "Porno for Pyros"
formerly the group "Jane's Addiction"
 "Nothing's Shocking"
with Perry Farrell
Dave Navarro on guitar
and Stephen Perkins
on drums
Ain't No Right they sing.
"What are you,
some kind of groupie?" I ask.
She says nothing.
Just turns up the volume.
Been Caught Stealing
they sing.

I hold her
Wet 'n' Wild lip gloss
diamond stud earrings
and glitter on her cheeks

Wan, she's looking wan
my dancing daughter

Hannah Davi —a new name—
walk-on in the movie *Day of Atonement*
with Christopher Walken

And a part in a Levitz Furniture ad
("it's work")
and a part in an MCI commercial
("Best Friends")
breaking in
Brotherhood Of Justice

a Swiss Alps bar-maid
("classic blonde Gretel")
in a Folger's Coffee commercial

"Grunge is in," she says
visiting Santa Cruz,
"any Goodwill's around?"

             *   *   *

Flashback

Appearing,
"crowning" says the doctor

"Hannah" says her mother
"the name means 'grace'"

Two-year-old drooling
as I toss her into space
and back
she falls
and back
into space again

Flawless teeth and perfect smile
one blue eye slightly larger than the other
her three-thousand miles away mother
still present as
two as one
two breathing together
we three breathe again as one
Hannah O Hannah

Take Me Home, I Need Repair

Take me home, I need repair. Take me please to anywhere.
—The Red Hot Chili Peppers
—For my son, Nicholas

He's a musician
Prophet
a raging Apollo
gold hoops,
diamond stud earrings
toenails and fingernails painted black

6'3", 200 pounds
legs propped up
on a wobbly stool

Listening
Magic-Red-Blood-Hot-Sugar
Chili-Sex

What I see is insanity.
Whatever happened to humanity?

"Good lyrics," I say

"The Chili Peppers," he says
"it's rap and it sucks.
Actually, I like Punk more—"

White steel guitar in hand
he demonstrates:

Fuck you... he sings.
End of demonstration.

Now he's Anthony Keidis
a tube sock
on his dick
One hot minute, and I'm in it...

Next he's trancey, anguished
Sonic Youth

Later:

Washing windows,
scrubbing floors,
dancing
doing
standup
impressions

My son the genie
my son Mr. Clean

Tries to jump into my arms.
Where do kids come from anyway?

"Fucking life
Everything sucks," he says

Mourning Kurt Cobain,
Hillel Slovak and the others
overdose dead.

Youthanasia

Whip-smart

Funk Da World
Funk Da World

I'm the father, I'm supposed to tell him—what?

"I know the truth," he says, "I know the truth."

Water Breather: Four For Michael

1. Swimmer in Air

Gulper of sea,
swimmer in air,

he dives, dives in again
again
water's
water,
air is air.

"Water's
water,
air is air,"
I say.
"No," he says, "no."

He's the breather of water,
three-year-old refuser,
won't be taught.

Intent, he makes his run,
big feet slapping, loopy leap
and sinks
to the bottom.

Swim to him.

"Water's
water," I begin...
he's red-eyed, sputtering, shaking—
Clambers up the ladder
to the dock
and jumps.

Scoop and hug him close
hold him out.

"Stroke, stroke
inhale
in air
exhale in water," I say,

"like this, Michael."
"Breathe in air, swim in water."

"No," he says, "no."

Slap, slap, his feet
on the side of the dock

He breathes in water
and swims in the air

breathes in water
and swims in air.

2. July 4

A boy achieves maximum pissing power
at age 5 or 6....
—Dr. Ed Jackson

"Michael, what the—"

six-year-old, dick in hand,
turning, his stream unbroken,

nine feet if it's an inch,
laughing, the kid's laughing
as he circles

360-degrees
hand all the time on the throttle,
slowly, back arched

he stands
"Dick, dink, decker,
weener, peter, pecker..." he sings
crowd gathering

nine feet from VW rooftop
to raging Mr. Beer-In-His-Hand.
"Is that your kid up there?"

I should laugh,
get up there with him,
lead our friends in applause.

"Dick, dink, decker," he sings,
face shining, joy to the world.

Rein him in, *do something,*
Jesus K. Christ,

"Dance," I want to say, "dance
on the roof of the German machine.

"Piss on, piss all you want—
What a stream!" I want to say.

Old fool, old scold,
too fearful to sing
"O Stream of Gold…"

Fucked father, fucked-up father,
I spank him instead.

3. House Boat

Lasqueti Island, B.C.

Washing dishes in the darkness
with a hose,
I spray off the few
remnants
of spaghetti onto the oysters

In their beds below.
Inside the single room
there is no running water—
only the green hose
on the deck of our floating home.

We secure the lines,
bathe and sing, *We all live in a Yellow Submarine...*
I reach out in the darkness
hearing my son brushing his teeth
to borrow his toothbrush.

I cannot find my own:
Tasting
my fourteen-year-old son's
mouth inside my mouth.
Then we find more dishes

And, as the moon rises and the lines
go tight,
continue scrubbing and drying silverware
and plates,
two dishwashers reading Braille.

4. Mountain Solitaire

i. Jerome, Arizona

He's thirty-two, my age
when he was born.
Haven't seen him for four years,
estranged son of estranged wife.

Phone:
"Please… leave… message…"
says the machine.
"Hey, Michael… It's Dad!"
He won't pick up, won't call back.

I court him, send gifts:
"Oh, boy, a cordless phone
from, let's see now, Mr. Walk-around…
my much-doodling daddy!"

I see him shake his head.
And write, I write him a poem.
Read it onto his answering machine.
"Dick, dink, decker,
weener, peter, pecker…"

He's away—a girlfriend
plays back the message.
"There's a stalker…" she tells him.
"No, that's my father," he says,
and calls me. He likes the poem.

ii. *Golden Gate Park*

We meet and he leads me
to the Hall of Flowers,
his dark hair combed forward,
bushing out over his ears,
single white strand glinting in the sun.

He's three, six and thirty-two;
I'm thirty-two, thirty-eight and sixty-four.
The prodigal father
and the abandoned 'live alone,'
Mr. Mountain Solitaire.

We stroll through the Garden of Fragrance,
oasis of lakes.

Absentee father
fathering,

he the fathered, fatherless
hungering

son to be a father
father to be father

This is the hunger.

—San Francisco, 1998

Sex & Tv with Aunt Miriam
New and Unpublished
1945

Part 1

"Always wash your hands after you've played in the backyard with those leaves and things before touching yourself," said my aunt, beginning our affair with this public service announcement.

"Yes, ma'am."

"Bobby, I'm going to show you how broadminded I am."

"Okay."

"But first I want you to tell me what you do with Lenore and her sister."

"Nuthin."

"You spin the bottle?"

"Yeah."

Luminous brown-eyed English Miriam abuzz with heat,
My left arm around her, my right hand
in her right hand
"Kiss me
love me
feel me, Bobby…"

I'm a pleaser. But… what was it she wanted me to do?

A seventh grader, I'd been held
back a year at school.
"He tries hard, and he's smart about some things, but…"
Anyway, I was right in there for a while with the slow learners.

Four thousand feet down in a North of England coal mine,
I'd just have grabbed a shovel and gotten to work.
I'd have known right away what to do.

Holding me with one hand, marking with the other,
D-I-C-K, wrote my twenty-something aunt.
Hmm. It felt good.

She finished by drawing some arrows and a bull's eye on her own body.

What was it like? It was like television, "informative and entertaining."
Never to have been fucked and never to have watched television either,
and then to be fucking *and* watching the evening news
on one of the first TVs in Chicago, and the Atomic
Bomb going off and the war over all at the same time, I think…
the truth is, I still don't understand.

The diagrams and the lettering helped.
I like seeing things labeled.
I'm so grateful.

"All art aspires to the state of music." That's true. I know that. And even at thirteen I loved Gershwin (*Rhapsody in Blue*), but I knew *real* music when I heard it. "O do me, thrill me." And *that's* what I went for. *That's* what I learned at thirteen. And *that's* what I'm grateful for.

O Miriam, say it again. Tell me where you want it. Draw me a picture.
Ah, dearest, how helpful it's been having those letters printed on my dick.

How many times have I been told,
"Bobby, you don't know your ass from a hole in the ground"?
More times than there are stars in the sky. And I hold my head high. At least I know where, O Aunt Miriam, O Miriam, to look for my dick.

*   *   *

Part 2

Fifty-two years later

"Oh, my God! I can't stand it," she said, hearing my voice.
"How *are* you, Bobby? I've been trying to find you. You're
a missing person, you know?"

"I write, I've even published," I said.

"I talked to that publisher of yours. Famous you're not."

"I know, I know. And what about you, Miriam?"

"I got some health problems. I go to temple, the *B'nai Brith*."

"And Uncle Jerry?"

"Dead. That's why I'm calling, Bobby. He's dead. Fifty-four
years
we'd been together." Uncle Jerry, the handsomest man in
Chicago,
circa 1945, singer on Chicago's WGN Radio.

"No one thought it would work. Fifty-four years and we yelled
all
the time. What does anyone know about anything?" she said.

"You stuck it out," I say. "That's good."

She's twenty-one, twenty-two,
pale, pinkie-brown where I put my lips.

"Enjoy yourself, Bobby. Life is to enjoy."
"What about Jerry? What about Uncle Jerry?"

"Listen to me. People go up and back between loving
and not loving.
Do you understand, Bobby?"

My lips here, there…
She's teaching me. "This is how you do it."

"See," she says, "see."
I'm thirteen and not wanting to. Then
wanting.

"I want to."

Woof, woof.

"That's Koko. That dog has a weight problem.
"She doesn't want to move.
"so I let her sleep on our bed.
"Koko is on morphine."

"Your dog is on morphine?"

"Did you ever hear of such a thing?
"Listen, you're all I got, Bobby.
"you're all the family that's left."

She wants me to fly to Chicago to see her.
"Do I have to draw you a picture?
"Come, Bobby. Come and see the sights."

We lie together… Betty Grable mouth
and red red lipstick
watching some old movie.
Listening at the same time to the radio.
It's the second half of a doubleheader.
Cubs versus the Pirates.
and the Cubs are ahead 4-3.

"That's good, Bobby. That's good.
"It's The Star Spangled Banner,
"O God, don't stop,
"It's The Stars and Stripes Forever.
"The Battle Hymn of the Republic.
"God Save the Queen!
"Do you understand?

"Don't stop."

She's pushing eighty, she says, and sells Avon. "It's a living."

I'm grateful, I want to say. I'm grateful for the arrows.
Whatever else has changed, I will always remember.

The aurora borealis,
and dawn's early light.
That was the year the Cubs won the pennant.

I understand, Miriam, these are the ties that bind.
Broad stripes and bright stars.
America the beautiful.
Purple mountains and spacious skies,
the screwed and sweetly screwy,
this our family, and this our country,

sweet land of liberty,
O fruited plain, O amber fields of grain,
from your apartment house to ours
('til Mom found out)
of thee, O darling, of thee I sing.

Millionaire

Grandpa Max, 1860-1958

1. His Inventions

Born in 1860, Austro-Hungarian immigrant,
inventor of a cap to keep the fizz
in seltzer bottles, a refinement to the machine gun,
and a metal Rube Goldberg bookmark
sold with a diagram and user manual,
Grandpa made big money speculating,
buying and selling tenements.
In the 1920s, offered stock in a start-up selling
flavored water and cocaine,
he turned it down. "Coca Cola," he spat.
"Vhat dreck! Who'd buy?"

2. His Economies

Lean, stiff-necked, pack-a-day smoker
with a fondness for syrupy wine, he wouldn't own a car,
used public transportation;
and, rather than buy toilet paper,
blackened his ass with yesterday's *Chicago Tribune.*

Grandpa never left a restaurant
—"vegetable soup, roll, glass of water"—
without pocketing a few cellophane-wrapped crackers
"for later."

At six, I got my first lesson in thrift.
Grandpa with a smoker's cough:
"Cough into four corners of hanky,
like this—
four coughs minimum—,
before you dirty up the middle."
End of lesson.

3. His Curses

Late summer afternoons, partaking of Mogen David
("Shield of David") wine,
he orbited the living room, sonofabitching
the government
and Democrats with no sense,
Franklin and Eleanor Roosevelt, "betrayers of the rich,
and they stole my patent, too."

God damning union leaders, *schnorrers,*
the United Mine Workers,
the AFL and CIO,
"Stand 'em up against a wall.
Shoot 'em, shoot the sons-a-bitches."

4. His Secret to Health and Long Life

Old Testament Moses,
cigarette and drink in hand,
white mustache, gray beard, pacing, pacing,
"God" (it was a prayer after all),
"damn" (the patriarch calling down wrath),
"son-a-bitch, son-a-bitch."
The last of his great inventions,
five syllables to God's four ("Let there be light"),
but good enough.
And that is how he'd breathe, cursing
—head back, chin up—everyone who, he figured,
had somehow cost him money.
"God damn son-a-bitch, God damn son-a-bitch!" he'd rage,
miraculously cured of whatever ailed him.

The Biggest Party Animal of Them All

The biggest party animal of them all
spoke Hindi, a little English,
suffered from diabetes,
was allergic to incense,
flowers and perfume,

loved chocolate,
gave it away, used it as *prasad*,
a gift to his disciples.

In his 70s he gave himself away,
reportedly 'poking' as many as 300
of his youngest followers.

'Now's your chance,' he'd say, his mouth full.
'That's right, child. Lie back,
meditate,' he'd croon. 'Have faith.'

The dude separated so many people from so much money
he had to create the Guru Om Foundation.
Rolls Royces, chauffeurs, ashrams in all the major cities.

The movement started small, twenty,
thirty,
then hundreds,
soon—

doctors, lawyers,
hoteliers, cocaine dealers and professors,
dancers, artists
and musicians
flocked to him,
himself a musician, masked actor, comic,
storyteller
extraordinaire.
Flatulent, potbellied old mystic,
giver-away of toys, party hats and favors to devotees.
The 'hundred-hatted yogi' we called him.

God, he was fun to be around!

Festivals with world-renowned performers,
dinner for five thousand,
and, afterwards,
we got to approach and touch his feet.

True, sometimes he'd flip out, become enraged,
have to be strapped down
or held,
one devotee at each limb.
Rudra the Howler.

Then, reviving,
'Chant.' 'Dance.' 'Meditate.'
Nataraj, the dancing Shiva, O graceful one!

Once, mid-revelry, irked by something I'd read aloud,
he drew back, swatted me four, five times
with a mass of peacock feathers. *Whoosh! Whoosh!*

It's known as *Shaktipat*, kick-start Kundalini yoga,
where the party thrower has only to touch someone—
blow to the head or soft caress—

and Zap!

For two, maybe three, minutes
I saw two worlds interpenetrating

jewels into jewels,
silver suns, electric whiteness,

World 'A' and world 'B'
one vibrating blue pearl,

world like a skyful of blue suns
Whoosh! Whoosh! Whoosh!

Head spinning, I began to laugh,
and he too, old cobra face,
began to howl,

mister three in one. Mister one in three.

O thou paunchy one
in Birkenstocks
and orange silk robe, trickster,
magician,
master cocksman,
hit me again!

Seven years I hung out with him,
even flew to India, meditated
in his cave
chanting to
scorpions, malaria mosquitoes
so illumined they chanted back.

phallic god,
god in the shape of a dick,
godfather
con man

killer god, god of death
and destroyer of all life

'Sonofabitch,' I say
'Sonofabitch!'
The guests are still arriving,
the party's just begun.

—*Oakland, California*

Fashion Makes the Heart Grow Fonder

Marriage and hanging go by destiny.
—Robert Burton, Anatomy of Melancholy

Partygoers
Her fruity, floral fragrance—
Honey at her dressing table
like a pilot in the cockpit,
a woman armed with old *TV Guides*, catalogs,
ordering information
for all the major scents and potions.

She put on (how can I describe them?)
refrigerator avocado green
and white
Keith Partridge bell-bottoms. Incandescent,
no less bizarre, I wore purple velveteen pants
and a tie-dyed shirt.

Her old lover Warren was there in his pimp suit,
giant bug-eye sunglasses
and huge fake fur pimp hat,
a party with vintage Joan Crawford movies,
Honey wearing Chanel Number 5,
the first synthetic scent.

And me, her consort, I wore
'a blend of crisp citrus and warm spice, mossy woods, a scent
for the feeling man.'

I remember her silver and turquoise earrings
on the make-up table
as the bed jumped and jerked
those first two years.

Ravi Shankar, Thai weed, and a little homegrown,
that velvet ribbon choker with butterflies
and the scent of Honey when she dropped her
tooled leather belt on the floor.

Then, "Tell me what you want," I said.
"You can't give me what I want."
"What do you want?"
"I'm out of style and so are you.
I want to lose weight."

And like that it was over.

"How about this handbag?" offered *Cosmo*,
"the perfect accessory
to the outfit you wear
when you leave your husband."

And that's how it ended. Honey at some fashion show
throwing back her head, the spotlight playing
on her face and neck.

Yes, I could see what Honey wanted,
to shop where she'd never shopped before,
to pull on high leather boots
and a mini-skirt; then, beaded Navaho handbag in hand,
flashing a little scented thigh, walking out on someone
who couldn't keep up,
a jerk in tie-dye.

I loved the woman, longed to stay with her and,
to do so, if I could have, arm-in-arm with her,
I'd have walked out on myself.

Post-Modern—A (Mostly) Found Poem*

"Joan of Arc was married to the Biblical Noah."
"The inhabitants of Egypt were called mummies,
and built pyramids in the shape of triangular cubes."

"The Pyramids are a range of mountains between France
and Switzerland."

He graded his papers
and went home to Honey.

"Areas of the dessert are cultivated by irritation."

Honey and the teacher were newlyweds.
Filing her nails, she watched some Joan Crawford movie.
Handed him a joint.

"Get your papers graded?" Applying nail polish,
Honey reached for *Cosmopolitan*,
turned back to the *TV Guide*.

All pink and red she was
and full of self-esteem and bounce,
teacher's fluorescent bride.

"Now or never," Honey said, her eyes twinkling,

"Post-civilization, post-modern, post-Cracker Jack,
early unforeseeable, post paradigm.

"Now you see it, now you don't."

"They lived in the Sarah Dessert and traveled by Camelot."

"In the dessert, the climate is such
the inhabitants have to live elsewhere."

"Come and get it," Honey called.
"Come and get it."

"In Europe, the enlightenment was a reasonable time."

With thanks to Richard Lederer's FRACTURED ENGLISH*

My Muse

As a rule, the power of absolutely falling in love soon vanishes... because the woman feels embarrassed by the spell she exercises over her poet-lover and repudiates it...
—Robert Graves, *The White Goddess*

"Why don't you just write a poem, right now?" she says.
'Western wind, when wilt thou blow...'
why don't you write a poem like that,
like that 'Anonymous'? Something inspirational."

"Talk about muses," I sulk,
"Yeats' wife was visited in her dreams by angels
saying, 'We have come to bring you images
for your husband's poetry.'"

"Yeah? So what?" she says. "It's out of style.
I already do too much for you."

Odalisque in a wicker chair,
book open on her lap,
dry Chardonnay at her side,
hand on a dozing, whiskered Sphinx.

"You need a muse," she says, "someone beautiful, mysterious,
some long-lost love,
fragile, a dancer perhaps. Look at me..."

"Yeah?" I say, refilling her glass,
"You hear me complaining? You're *zaftig*."
"Zaftig?"
"Firm, earthy, juicy, too," I say.

*   *   *

"Juicy plum," I say, in bed, left hand over her head,
"rose petals," I say, right arm around her.
"Silver drop earrings," I murmur, ordering out
for gifts. "Aubergine scarf, gray cashmere cardigan."

I do this in my sleep. Go shopping in my sleep.
"Oh, yeah, and a case of Chardonnay."
Wake to the scent of apple blossoms,
decades in the glow of rose light.

*   *   *

"Wake," she whispers. I tell her my dream.
We kiss. Poppy Express. Racy Red. Red Coral.
Star Red.
Red red.

"Enough. That's enough," she says.

Amnesia

Somewhere an ocean of doorknobs,
a cemetery for seaweed.

The sailors,
all of them,
walking
at
some slight angle
counter to the angle
everyone else
walks at.
The ships and the rain
Slanting
at still
another
angle.
And music
and the woman
one has children by
bears her child
and her belly
every day
at a different
angle.

We are under water
Come up and the surf is filled with rooftops, planes overhead
narrowly missing trees, it begins raining upwards.

Things get lonely to go outside.
Sometimes the body gets lonely to go outside.
Sometimes everything and the body also goes outside
at once.

Every morning at precisely that moment
the woman asks for his dreams,
he has none,
or forgets or wants to forget or
conceives he is dying.
In his memory
they break up
almost entirely
because he can not
remember his dreams.
On the other hand, she remembers hers
and tells them
compulsively.

He reads bed sheets. Imprint of lines. The woman's neck.
The word "Mother" tattooed somewhere. A cluster of red
freckles above the "M." She sits up and yawns.
"I want," she says, "I want."

The House on Stilts

Cross Lake, Wisconsin - Illinois 1950

There is no sleep, this night
in me, in the room
where I write my sleep.
I open the window, and unhook
the screen; the bushes, metal lawn chairs
streetlamps
the moon, pieces of a living room.

Stilts, rotted long pilings,
stand just beneath the bookcase, TV,
bedroom and kitchen,
the four corners of the house.

The sky,
a starry imitation ceiling—
our family, propped,
house-on-stilts people,
goiter, bulgy-eyed mother,
weekend father,
half in one state, half in
another
and dashes on the map,
Cross Lake with a line
running through it.

*   *   *

The highway alive, aloud
a blatant strip of rug.
And people,
in their houses,
the back doors opening, slamming.

Every hour
someone screams quietly for a while.
And babies, in little closed windows.
The TV, a bluish, fluorescent hearth.

–Tilting, facing
its double, the house on stilts.

A house in the shape, a dream
in the shape, of itself
of its house, of its dream.

A sleep
the impossibility of sleep,
the vision, the life that it requires.
Her eyes opening, singing,
my mother, former Miss Chicago,
on a springboard.

Heavenly Sex
Black Moss Press
2002

One for the Road

One for the road.
A little detached it was, but bouncy, flouncy, hoochie coochie,
woo wah woo, out there under the stars,
woo wah woo,
one for the road, one for the road it was,
and end of the show.
Stupid shit, how was I to know?
One for the road and end of the show?
So good-humored it was, I missed the clue,
hugging and kissing, all that
hugging and kissing.
Missed just how all over it really was.

Turning 60

The first 40 years of life give us the text;
the next 30 supply the commentary on it...
—Schopenhauer

1. Homework

According to Webster, the word six derives from the Latin
"sex" [s-e-x] and the Greek "hex" [h-e-x].
Six units or members
as, an ice-hockey team;
a 6-cylinder engine;
six fold, six-pack, sixpenny nail, six-
shooter, sixth sense.

"Zero" denotes the absence of all magnitude, the point of departure
in reckoning; the point from which the graduation of a scale
(as of a thermometer) begins;
zero hour,
zeroth,
as, "the zero power of a number."

Zero, the great "there's nothing there" number,
a blast off into a new decade.

2. Grammar as Hymnal

Seeking solace in a review of grammar, I turned to Strunk & White's
ELEMENTS OF STYLE. Standing at attention,
opening to the section on usage, I chanted and sang –
uniting my voice with the voices of others, the vast chorus
of the lovers of English.

We sing of verb tense, past, present and future.
We sing the harmony of simple tenses.
We lift our voice in praise of action words,
and the function of verb tense.

We sing of grammar which is our compass
providing, as it does, clues as to how
we might navigate the future,
at the same time it
illuminates the past.

As a teacher, I talk. That's present.
For thirty years as a teacher, I talked. That's past.
It may only be part time, but I will talk. That's future.

3. Living the Future Perfect

I will have invoked the muse.

I will have remembered to give thanks, knowing our origins
are in the invisible, and that we once possessed boundless energy,
but were formless, and that we are here to know 'the things of the
heart
through touching.'

I will have remembered, too, that there is only one thing
we all possess equally and that is our loneliness.

I will have loved.
You will have loved.
We will have loved.

God Is In The Cracks, A Narrative in Voices
Black Moss Press
2006

Author's Note

At the heart of *God Is In The Cracks* is my Talmud-conversant father, of Russian-Jewish extraction —a Chicago-based podiatrist by profession—who came unhinged after my mother's death at age 42.

In the late 40s he became a Rosicrucian and practiced his rites secretly in the basement of our home. Dad evolved his own blend of kabbalistic, Christian hermetic, and prescient New Age mysticism which lent its colors to his medical practice as well as to his view of my eventual career choice and several marriages.

This book draws on *Rosicrucian In The Basement* and *Heavenly Sex* (Black Moss Press) and includes a dozen new poems in the father-son series. The poems here are sequenced to form a narrative spanning 60 years (1945 to present) and are best read in the order printed.

Getting Through the Night

The Podiatrist's Son

When our feet hurt, we hurt all over.
—Socrates

    Feet is Feet, Putz is Putz

Mother:
"The boy has urges.
He's at that age."

Father:
"So?"

"*Shh.* Talk to him, you're a doctor."

"A podiatrist, not a *putzmeister.*"

"Please, say something."

"Feet is feet, *putz* is *putz.*
I'll buy him a book."

"Sit already! Breakfast,
sweet rolls, coffee…
Oi, there he is now, sneaking up on us,
Mr. Secrets
with the half-open eyes, see?
But the mouth, that he keeps shut.
And he scribbles, *oi!*
scribble, scribble, scribble
he's a *shlimazel.*"

"He's a dreamer."

"But unlucky. You know what it means, son,
shlimazel?
From the German, *shlim*, 'bad' it means,
and *mazel*, this even you know, 'luck.'
So, *shlimazel*,
you look into the river,
the fish drop dead.
You deal in shrouds,
people stop dying.
Now you know. Now you know *shlimazel.*"

"*Shlimazel?* Unlucky?
Better you think
we shouldn't have a son?
The boy's a dreamer,
he makes things up.
But look, his feet still
aren't on the ground"

"They've never been on the ground.
Dreamer, *schemer…* Listen to me, son,
one day you'll wake up,
come down to earth
and become a doctor, a real doctor.
Get educated, get married, get out—
Make your mother proud of you."

"He's round-shouldered.
He walks with his head down. See?
And he toes in.
Poor feet, poor posture.
He's a dreamer. The boy lives
in another world."

"A therapist he should see."

"So, we're made of money?"

"Money? Two nurses you have, *shiksas* no less,
x-ray machine, whirlpool, diathermy,
a hospital doesn't have such equipment.
A therapist he should see,
but shoes we can afford."

"That's it, Oxfords,
Florsheims, shoes
that will support him,
shoes with laces,
shoes that breathe."

"Listen, listen to your father."

2. How To Shop For Shoes

Seymour Shoes, Maxwell Street, Chicago

"No loafers, no sandals, nothing
without laces."

"There are fifty-two bones in the feet;
thirty-three joints; more than one
hundred tendons, muscles and
ligaments…"

"Fit for length, fit for width,
 get both feet fitted.

"People are asymmetrical. You'll find
one foot, one testicle, one breast
larger than the other…"

"Listen, listen to your father."

"Feet swell, grow larger
as the day goes on.

"So, *nu?* shop when they're bigger,
  shop for the larger foot.

"Otherwise…
heel pain, heel spurs, bunions and
hammertoes…

"Remember, there's no 'break-in period,'
shoes don't break in.
Buy what feels right now."

"Born in *shtetl*,
now here he is, a doctor."

3.Getting Through the Night

"So: the foot is the mirror of health.
What's that smell?
Let me see your feet. *Oi!*

"How many times do I have to say it?
A pair of feet have 25,000 sweat glands,
can produce eight ounces, a cup of perspiration in a single day.

"One quarter of all the bones in the
human body are in the feet."

He sits at my bedside carving arch supports.

"Take a flashlight.
Never walk around in the dark.
Most foot fractures occur at night…

"Now remember your slippers," he says
as I head for the bathroom.

In my father's house, there are no bedtime stories.

Son of the Commandment

Chicago

"So, twelve years old! Soon you'll be *bar mitzvah*,
a *mensch*, a human being. Yes, son,
a human being, you. 'Today I am a man,' you'll say,
like I did. Let's see what you know:
The serpent in the Bible, what language does he speak?

"What's wrong with you? He speaks Hebrew. Same as God.
Same as Abraham and Isaac.
Same as Jesus.
Who else speaks Hebrew?

"Adam and Eve. Noah, too, and the animals:
the giraffe, the kangaroo, the lion.
Hebrew.

Hebrew.
Soon you'll speak Hebrew.
Yes, and you'll read it too. *Apostate!*

"You're going to Hebrew School.

"Why? So you can speak to God in His own language.
Lesson One: *Bar* means son, *mitzvah* means commandment.
Bar mitzvah: Son of the commandment.
Commandment, *mitzvah*: What God gave to Moses.

"Lesson Two: When did Jews get souls?

"Souls they got when they got *Torah*.
Torah. Torah is Commandments.
Torah is soul.

"So learn, *bar mitzvah* boy! Read. Learn the blessing.
Do it right and you'll see
the letters fly up to heaven.

"Learn. Yes. There's money
in puberty,
money in learning. Books, money, fountain
pens… Always remember: learning is the best merchandise.
"Lesson Three: *Daven* means pray. You rock back and forth
like the rabbi,
and pray. In Hebrew.
From your mouth to God's ear.
But it has to be in Hebrew.
And you can't mispronounce:
And no vowels to make it easy."

What Was God Thinking?

1. At the Hospital

Father:
"I don't understand. What was God thinking,
what was He thinking?"

Mother:
"What's to understand?
I'm dead.
We weren't made to last.
What's to understand?
Ach, he doesn't hear me."

"God forgive me.
A good woman. At least may she rest in peace."

"Rest in peace? I'm dead for god sake.
What good will rest do?
You rest in peace.
And something else, my friend, no viewing,
no 'open casket.' They want to look at me, let them
go look at someone else. Later,
if they want to visit, fine.
They know the address.
But no flowers. Tell them. No flowers.
Flowers die.
Stones they should bring, not flowers.
And as for afterlife, tell them, there is no 'afterlife.'
Look at him. He doesn't hear a word I'm saying."

2. The End of the World

"He stripped your mother, son,
stripped the soul from her body.
You think a human life is not a world?
So then mourn,
mourn for the end of the world.
And cover the mirrors.
Oi, look at you:
Take off those shoes.
This is not a time for leather.
Here, let me tear that shirt for you.
Why? Because your mother's dead. God did her in;
her death should cost you something too.
That's right and put ashes on your head.
You're sitting *shiva* now.
It's the law. You're a Jew.
Read the small print.
Seven days you cannot leave the house.
No radio, no TV, no looking at magazines,
no books.
You'll see what death is like.
She's gone, so mourn, damn you, mourn!"

Kaddish

May the Great Name be blessed...

1. Mother's Limousines

"Mourn like a Jew," Grandfather Max says,
tearing my shirt
from the collar down,
"and when she's buried, rip out the grass
and wail.
Expose your heart. Lament for her."

Mother, mother
mother of the inflamed heart.

Car door slamming behind us as we exit...

Bar-mitzvah'd boy, 14, I say it once,
say what I'm told to say,
"He is the Rock, His work is perfect..."
Say it,
YIT-GA-DAL
V'YIT-KA-DASH
SH'MEI
RA-BA
B'AL MA...
the Kaddish of sounds, not words

"May a great peace from heaven..." I say,
"May His great Name be blessed,
...Magnified and sanctified...
Y'HAY
SH'LAMA
RA-BA
MIN SH'MAYA
V'CHAYIM
 ALENU... I say.

...a week later,
no to the rabbi,
no to morning,
no to twilight,
no to the mid-day prayer
no repeating the prayer three times a day for a year
no, I say, and no to the *shul*.

"We're animals first and human second," she says, "and there is no
God. Do you hear me?"

Fox-trotting mother. Dancer mother. Beauty Queen
in the house of prayer.

"Mom," I ask, "how do you pray?"
She shakes her head and turns away.
 "Snap out of it," she says.

"Better to go shopping," she says,
"better to get a job, better to make money."
I reach out. "Mom—"

"Hands off," she says, "hands off."

"Kids," she says. "*Oi vay*."
"Holocaust," she says. "*Oi, oi, oi*."
"God," she says. "What God?"

"Bless the Lord who is blessed," I don't pray.
"May the Great Name be blessed," I don't pray,
but burn a candle so Mother,
Miss Chicago,
can find her way back.

Later, I cannot recall her face.
"…you're not to look on any photo of her,
not for seven days," says Grandfather.
What did she even look like?
Faceless son
mourning a faceless mother,
mourning her,
mourning
freelance,
mourning on the fly.

"She'll wander for seven days," Grandfather says,
"then, when she's wormed, her soul will return to God."

lacks a body and I can't recall her face
lacks a body and I can't recall her face

"Save her soul from *Gehenna*.
Join us," pleads the rabbi.
No, no is my prayer
No to duty and no to prayer.

Who was she? Some brunette rich girl
I never knew,
a stranger dead at 42.
Mother, the beautiful secretary.
I touch her in a dream. She turns,
and there's no one there.

I shake from head to foot.
I stand and I sway.
"Mother, Mother," I say.

Blessed be the stranger.
No, no to the stranger,
no to the stranger.

No is my Kaddish.
No is my prayer.
I am the no
I am the not.

I will not be her savior,
I will not.

2. Gehenna, or Purgatory

Mother applies Pond's Beauty Cream. Her face glistens. Massages
her forehead with one hand,
holds the other to her heart.

"What's the point?" she asks, cigarette ablaze,
mouth tightening.

When she dies, they bury her not in a shroud, but in pancake make-up
and best gray dress.

"Turn the photos to the wall," says Grandfather,
"and cover your lips.

That's right. Now cover your face.
Isolate yourself — groan — let your hair grow wild.
The mourner is the one without a skin, says the Talmud.
Understand? You are no longer whole."
And I think: *I am going to die, too.*

Sit in silence and say nothing.

"How about a prayer to locusts?" I pray,
"How about a prayer to boils?

"O murdering heaven," I pray.

Grandfather cooks lentils,
lentils and eggs. "Mourners' food," he calls it.

*"A prayer to rats,
and a prayer to roaches."*

"Death is the mother of beauty," he says.
"The death of another makes you want to die," he says.
"The Angel of Death is made entirely of eyes," Grandfather says.

Damn seeing,
Damn touching.
Damn feeling.
Damn loving.

In Jewish hell—
I am the unknowing,
the not Jewish Jew.

Split, cloven,
cracked
In hell

nameless,
and eyeless,
faceless.

No, no to blessings,
no to teachings,
no to reading from right to left.

I pray with them,
I pray with the no, I pray with the not.
I pray with the dead, I pray with the damned.

God, God who is a wound, we pray.

3. Against Darkness

"Kaddish is a song against darkness," says the rabbi.
YIT-GA-DAL
V'YIT-KA-DASH
SH'MEI
RA-BA
B'AL MA...
"'Magnified and sanctified
May His Great Name Be...'
No it says, no to darkness. No to nothingness.
'May His Great Name be blessed.'
Kaddish praises God...
Kaddish: a mourner's prayer
that never mentions death.
Y'HAY
SH'LAMA
RA-BA
MIN SH'MAYA
V'CHAYIM...

"Now then, Let R__, the son of G__,
come forward," says the rabbi,
but I freeze, pretend not to hear.
Again he calls, calls me to say Kaddish.
(Loudly) "Let R__, son of G__, step beside me."
Ten other mourners turn in my direction.

Again I pretend not to hear.
Staring, face crimson, then white, he turns
and continues with the service.

The Lord is our God, the Lord is One...
I mourn her — mourn Kaddish — mourn *shul*
and head for home. Age 14, I walk out
looking
for stones
I might hurl into heaven.

*   *   *

I am the un-*bar'd mitzvah*,
escaped
Jew from nowhere,
apostate,
skipped Jew,
cleft Jew,
Jew, pause in the beating of the heart.

*   *   *

Once home, I pray, "Damn Him,
"damn G-d," I pray.

*   *   *

Mother, car door slamming,
the shovel biting
Mother, whose body is the world,
spinning into space—

"Life rattles," she says.
"My son, His Royal Highness," she says,
"get used to it."

"Mom, is there an afterlife?"
"Shape up," she says. "You are my afterlife.
God help us."

4. Anniversary

"We're just subdivisions of one person.
One's no better than any other.
Someone dies and you move forward
into the front lines," Grandfather says,
lighting a *yortzeit* candle.

"'Blessed art thou who raises the dead...'"

Shaking the match, he turns. *"Gottenyu!"* he says.
"I should have been next."
Tears well up
and I see him see her
in me.

"Same color hair,
same eyes..." Grandfather says.
"Remember seeing her in her coffin?" he asks,
grabbing my arm.
"Your mother didn't believe, but she'll be raised
and rest with G-d. Does love quit?

"Can you feel her... hear her inside you?"
I nod.
"Where?"
"Here, in my chest."
"And what does she say?"
"She says nothing," I reply,
but she does:
"Loopy doop," she says, *"Rest in peace!*
Wait'll you die, you'll see. There is no peace. When you're dead,
you're dead.
Enough.
Meshugge!" she says, and shakes her head.

"Pray, damn you," he says. "It's your mother."

"…Now it's over," he sobs.
 "But you, the un-mourner
will mourn for her all your life.

"Jew, Jew without beginning," he mocks,
"Jew who got away."

The School of Light

1. Science of the Unseen

"Son, did you know wood decays
at the same rate as the human body?
So what's the good of a casket?
What's the good of a body?
Go, go without sleep!
Goddammit,
it makes you crazy.
Read, then. Read this Rosicrucian.
The wise man sees in Self those that are alive
and those that are dead.
Yeats, Yeats,
you should read *The Rose.*
For me now, it's back to school. The inner college.
It's a brotherhood, it's science,
College of the Unseen, but science.
Roses and crosses. *Ach*, you've seen the ad.
Then you've seen the eye of God.
So I wrote away. They sent me this.
Beauty. Splendor.
Mercy. Wisdom.
It's not Jewish, but you think it's not Jewish?
It's not so not Jewish.
Nightmares. Your dead mother. *Oi.*
A man needs to get through the night."

2. Fraternity of the Earth

"'Beyond the point where nothing is known
is called The Beginning.
Within The Beginning, the Unknown created God.'
Talmud says. And this they teach,
the Rosicrucians.
Over here, son, can you smell?
Roses, roses and incense…
the aroma of infinity.
Ach, what would you know?
You, you think it's easy?
Burlap bags she patched,
so we could eat.
And could she read, your grandmother?
In *shtetl,* in Poltava, who could read?
But look, *The Chicago Tribune, Popular Mechanics*…
Here, an ad again, the School of Light, see?
'Holiness pervades physical matter.'
And you, questions, questions…
'What is Rosicrucian? What is Rosicrucian?'
A fraternity, a brotherhood…
Enough. She's dead, your mother, I need this.
A man needs to get through the night."

3. A Trip to the Zoo

"Lead into gold, easy!
But I need a fraternity,
that's right, a fraternity.
Brotherhood,
the Fraternity of the Earth.
Why? To learn the language, do the alchemy.
Here, I'm going to pull an eyelash.
Now, under a microscope...
mites, bacteria, fungi, see?
I'm your father, but what am I? A zoo.
You're my son, but what are you? Also, a zoo.
Yes, there's a universe in a grain of sand,
a father—10,000 fathers—
and sons too
in this one eyelash.
So, as many creatures on our bodies
as there are universes, as there are fathers, as there are zoos,
zoos, zoos, and the zoos of zoos.
You think you're alone?
Here, son, a Rosicrucian eyelash."

Anniversary of Her Death

At the Rosicrucian Altar

Sweeps away incense and candles,
liquid-filled crystal flask…
"Forget prayer, forget everything I ever said."
Bolts the door, pours himself a drink.

Said about what, dad?

"What? Prayer. *Everything*. Forget it!
God doesn't need your prayer.
Now put on your shoes and get out of here."

But dad, this stuff is just beginning
to make sense.

"Nonsense," he says.

What about the unseen?

"Goddammit, if it isn't seen,
it isn't there.
She's dead. Your mother's dead.
What are you, stupid?"
Reaches for matches. Lights a cigarette.

But what about… soul?

"Soul? You know better than that.
There is no soul."

And 'the other side'?

"There is no other side. You want to know
what's on the other side? Nothing.
That's what's on the other side.
Ach, you're looking for meaning.
Meaning's on backorder.
The sun and the moon and the stars,
they're all on backorder.
Nothing's there. Nothing ever existed.
She's dead. Don't you get it? The world is just a word.
Talmud says.
Earth is a flaming word.
That's it. That's it. End of story."

ii

Jew Overboard

Lenore and the Leopard Dog

Father's heart attacks him.

1. Catahoula Leopard Dog

Lenore K. appears at our door.
Father greets her. He wears
a silk bathrobe,
big horn-rimmed glasses
and his eyes bob up and down;
"I'm feeling better…"

You better be better.

Lenore shakes out her shoulder-length,
silvery-blond hair.
Poppa's eyes widen. Heart attack or no heart attack,
he's ready. Already he's ready.

LOOK, ALREADY HE'S READY, says Leopard Dog,
racing room to room, one brown eye,
one blue eye, sizing me up.
LIKE IT OR NOT, SONNY, WE'RE HERE TO STAY.

Oh, why, hello there, Sonny.
I'm Daddy's new friend.
And that, that meshugge
is a Catahoula Leopard Dog… see the spots?
And smart. He understands everything.

"A handsome wife develops the mind of man," Father says.

"No, please, dad," I whisper, "I don't want her,
I don't want another mother."

He cups my face
in his hand.
"Goddammit, I've told you, it's not good
for a man to be alone. And you need a mother."

Leopard dog wags his tail. *WOOF, WOOF*. Stands
on his hind legs, paws on my shoulders.
WE'RE MOVING IN, FARSHTEHST?
Springs across the room, switches on
I Love Lucy.

Lenore sets the table.

*What a dog! He just loves television. Mmm…
that Ricky Ricardo, look at those yummy
bedroom eyes.*

Shh, says Father.

*You told me yourself, God is right there
in the pleasure. O, you're good, doctor,
you're good, she whispers.*

2. *The Mystery of the Mouth*

Later that night

"Your breasts are like twins, young roes
which feed
among the lilies."

Leopard Dog and I listen at the door.

What are you talking about, honey?

AH, HERE COME THE BIRDS AND BEES, says Dog.

"It's in the Bible. A woman's breasts
are the Ten Commandments, the two tablets
of God's law. One for what God allows,
one for what He doesn't."

Talk sense. You're a doctor, she laughs.

I peek through the keyhole.

Father's kneeling by the bed, pouring wine.

What about kissing?

"Kissing is praying too, darling. Look, I bow my head,
same as when I pray."

"They make me sick," I say.

"I've told you before, dear, God rewards you for kissing."

Lenore sits up in bed. *Whaa—?*

"The way we make love is the way God will be with us.
With the mouth alone it is possible. That's right, darling,
that's the mystery of the mouth."

Leopard dog wags his tail.
THIS IS GOOD, he says.

"Shut up. You're a stupid dog," I say. "What do you know?"

I KNOW YES AND NO
AND *BOW WOW*. GOOD DOG,
BAD DOG. I KNOW PLAY
AND STAY. LICK I KNOW
AND SNIFF I KNOW. *BOW WOW*,
BOW WOW, WHAT DO YOU KNOW?

"Who's that?" Father yells.

That's just Leopard. He knows we're in here.
He's lonely. Darling, would you mind?
He likes to watch.

"What?"

You know what I'm saying. He's just a dog.

3. *The Holiness in Sex*

GR-R-R— Leopard on his haunches
peeping through the keyhole.

"Hey, move over, Dog, scram!"

Leopard Dog snaps at my hand,
eyes like cracked glass.

LOOK OUT. I EAT LITTLE BOYS FOR BREAKFAST!

"The socks come off and the feet talk," Father says.

YOUR FATHER'S ALL MUSCLE.
WHO WOULD HAVE THOUGHT?
LENORE LIKES THAT. THEY'RE A MATCH.
THAT'S YOUR NEW MOTHER.

"The way to heaven is not up, but down.
Love—marriage—intercourse, what are they, darling?
A tangling of toes, right?
So, how does this feel, Lenore?
Good… and this?"

Oh, doctor, doctor… You know,
I like professional men… full of surprises.
Crazy talk. Silly exams… touching…
and nice pajamas.

THERE THEY GO, SONNY.

"The holiness derives from feeling the pleasure," Father says.
"No pleasure, no holiness."

OOO, WICKY, WICKY, says Leopard Dog,
THAT'S HOW YOU WERE MADE, LITTLE BOY.
NO WICKY WICKY, NO LITTLE BOY.

"Move, darling, move, you need to move!"

LOOK AT THAT. IT'S HEELS OVER BEDPOSTS.
IT'S WICKY WICKY HE LOVES, NOT YOU, SONNY.

4. Lenore Gets on Top

Father sits on the side of the bed
whinnying like a horse.
That lady does it too.

"So look at us," he says,
reaching for her.
"we're invisible, that's what we are."

Invisible?

"Invisible, yes: no boundary between exterior and interior.
Tell me, darling, where do I leave off and you begin?
Inside you is inside me. Outside you is outside me.
We're both the same.
So, *nu*, who sees that? Who sees us? We're invisible."

Luftmensch, head in the clouds.
You miss this, doctor, and you miss that.
You think that makes you a mystic?
Invisible? I'll show you invisible.

WHAT, YOU STILL DON'T GET IT? says Dog,
thwacking me with his tail.
LENORE'S YOUR MOMMY, LITTLE BOY;
WICKY WICKY'S YOUR FATHER.
YOU HAD A MOTHER.
NOW YOU HAVE ANOTHER.

Hands on his shoulders, she sits on father,
moves up and down.

Now you see it, now you don't, she says.

BAD LENORE, BAD. THAT'S NOT DOG, says Dog,
barking at the keyhole.
 "There is man and woman and a third thing, too,
in us, says the poet. That's the eye in the heart
that sees into the invisible. The goal, Poet says, is to see
with the eye of the heart so like sees like."

Shut up, she says, *shut up and schtupp.*

"Oh God, marry me," he says, "marry me."

Rosicrucian in the Basement

i

"What's to explain?" he asks.
He's a closet meditator. Rosicrucian in the basement.
In my father's eyes: dream.
"There are two worlds," he says,
liquid-filled crystal flask
and yellow glass egg
on the altar.
He's the "professional man"—
so she calls him, my stepmother.
That, and "the Doctor":
"The Doctor will see you now," she says,
working as his receptionist.
He's a podiatrist—foot surgery a specialty—
on Chicago's North Side.
Russian-born Orthodox Jew
with *zaftig* Polish wife, posh silvery white starlet
Hilton Hotel hostess.

ii

This is his secret.
This is where he goes when he's not making money.
The way to the other world is into the basement
and he can't live without this other world.
"If he has to, he has to," my stepmother shrugs.
Keeps door locked when he's not down there.
Keeps the door locked when he is.
"Two nuts in the mini-bar," she mutters, banging pots
in the kitchen upstairs.
Anyway, she needs to protect the family.
"Jew overboard," she yells, banging dishes.
"Peasant!" he yells back.

iii

"There are two worlds," he says lighting incense, "the seen
and the unseen, and she doesn't understand.
This is my treasure," he says,
lead cooking in an iron pan,
liquid darkness and some gold.
"Son, there are three souls: one, the Supernal;
two, the concealed
female soul, soul like glue…
holds it all together…"
"And the third?" I ask.
We stand there, "I can't recall."
He begins to chant and wave incense.
No *tallis*, no *yarmulke*,
just knotty pine walls and mini-bar
size of a ouija board,
a little schnapps and shot glasses
on the lower shelf,
and I'm no help.
Just back from seven thousand dollar trip,
four weeks with Swami Muktananda,
thinking
Now there's someone who knew how to convert
the soul's longing into gold.
Father, my father: he has this emerald tablet
with a single word written on it
and an arrow pointing.

What's to Explain?

2. Jesus

"What's with the cross? You believe in Jesus, dad?"
"What?"
"Are you still a Jew?"
He turns away.
"Dammit, it's not a religion, *farshtehst?*"
Brings fist down on the altar.
"We seek the perfection of metals," he says,
re-lighting stove,
"salvation by smelting."

"But what's the point?" I ask.

"The point? Internal alchemy, *shmegegge. Rosa mystica,*" he shouts.
Meat into spirit, darkness into light."

Seated now, seated on bar stools.
Flickering candle in a windowless room.
Visible and invisible. Face of my father
in the other world.
I see him, see him in me
my rosy cross
podiatrist father.
"I'm making no secret of this secret," he says,
turning to the altar.
"Tell me, tell me how to pray."
"Burst," he says, "burst like a star."

3. Rosy Cross Father

"Yes, he still believes. Imagine—
American Jews,
when they die,
roll underground for three days
to reach the Holy Land.
He believes that."

We're standing at the Rosicrucian mini-bar listening,
(clash of pots in the kitchen upstairs)
father
with thick, dark-rimmed glasses
blue-denim shirt,
bristly white mustache,
dome forehead.

"Your stepmother's on the phone with her sister," he says.

"He thinks he can look into the invisible,"
she says from above.
"He thinks he can peek into the other world,
like God's out there waiting for him…
Meshugge!"

She starts the dishwasher.

"As above, so below," he says.
"I'm not so sure," I say.
"Listen, everyone's got some stink," he says,
grabbing my arm,
"you think you're immune?"
I shake my head.

"To look for God is to find Him, " he says.
 "If God lived on earth," she says, "people would knock out
all His windows."

"Kibbitzer," he yells back. *"Gottenyu! Shiksa brain!"*

Father turns to his "apparatus,"
"visual scriptures," he calls them,
tinctures and elixirs,
the silvery dark and the silvery white.

"We of the here-and-now, pay our respects
to the invisible.
                  Your soul is a soul," he says, turning to me,
"but body is a soul, too. As the poet says,
'we are the bees of the golden hive of the invisible.'"
"What poet, Dad?"
"The poet! Goddammit, the poet," he yells.

He's paler these days, showing more forehead,
thinning down.

 "We live in darkness and it looks like light.
Now listen to me: I'm unhooking from the world, understand?
Everything is a covering,
contains its opposite.
The demonic is rooted in the divine.
Son, you're an Outside," he says,
"waiting for an Inside.
but I want you to know…"
"Know what, Dad?"
"I'm gonna keep a place for you in the other world."

Rosicrucian One-Dollar Bill

"Franklin was a Rosicrucian.
He made it. He made
the one-dollar bill.
Open your wallet, take out a dollar.
Money talks, in pictures
it talks. See,
Egyptian pyramid.
Money, American money
with a pyramid.
The eagle, that you understand,
thunderbolts in one hand,
olive branch in the other.
So, the pyramid,
what does *that* say?
'You have no idea,' it says,
'you don't know the value of money.
Money is to remind you
what's important in life.' Look:
see, a halo with lines...
above the pyramid,
'Glory,' that's what they call it,
a 'Glory,' burst of light
with the eye of God inside.
But the pyramid is unfinished, it needs work, like you.

"'*Ach*, enough! Enough with money,' says money.
Just remember, God has His eye on you.
And the sun and the moon and the stars are inside you.
So listen, listen to the pyramid.
You can't buy your way into heaven, it's true,
but you need to know money to get there.'"

Marriage 1, 2, 3, 4

Heavenly Sex

1. The Law

Opens a bottle of schnapps. "Writer, *schmyter*,
you're unemployed.
Unemployed people must make love
at least once a day.
Talmud says:
A laborer, twice a week; a mule driver
once a week; a camel driver,
once a month. It's the law.
This is heavenly sex. Say a blessing—
pray— 'Blessed art thou, O Lord our God…'
Ba-ruch a-ta…
For your spouse and for your seed.
What is it with you?
I need to explain how to bring a soul into the world?"

2. The Blessing

"Listen:
The soul is the Lord's candle.
So you say a blessing. And you sing to her—your wife:
Strength and honor are her clothing, you sing.
She opened her mouth with wisdom, you sing.
Her children arise up and call her blessed, you sing.
Rabbi says if knowing a woman were not holy,
it would not be called 'knowing.'
So, after a good *Shabbes* meal—
linen tablecloth, blessed spices,
braided loaves of *challah,*
a goblet of wine…
Thirty-nine things you cannot do on the Sabbath,
but you can eat. You can drink. You can *schtupp.*
Make one another happy.
It's the law."

The Podiatrist Pronounces
on His Son's Divorce

"The time for sorry is past.
When a Jew gets divorced, even the altar sheds tears.
Rabbi says.
Look at these X-rays, perfect daughter.
Her feet we can fix. This is not a problem.
Perfect little girl,
just a little knock-kneed.
My God, this is your daughter, a daughter
you're leaving! Five thousand steps a day women take.
Fifty thousand miles in a lifetime. Where will that take her?
And where will you be?
Other people He created from the feet up
and at the end they get a brain.
But you it's the other way around—and He forgot the feet.
All these years, all these years, and you got nothing on the ground.
In this life there are two things, son:
Children and money,
and in that order. What else?
Ach, so leave, leave if leaving is what you're going to do.
You're not going anywhere.
Truth is, you're not going anywhere anyway."

Wedding #2

1. Temple Parking Lot

Father, removing glasses:
"So, my son is getting married!"

For the second time, dad.

"Yes, but weddings heal. Our Talmud says
 a wedding frees bride and groom
from all past transgressions.
A wedding fixes all that's broken."

You mean one marriage can fix another?

He grabs my arm: "A happy marriage
gives eternal dispensation."

His eyes gather light.
"The Talmud says intercourse is one-sixtieth
the pleasure of paradise."

I'm wearing five-eyelet Florsheims
with new arch supports.

"This is good." He waves to friends.
"Just don't fumble the goblet."

The goblet?

"The goblet you break after the vows.
This time use your heel. Smash it on the first try.
People'll be watching. Miss it and they'll laugh—
like last time.
Don't fumble the goblet."

2. Temple Steps

Leads with his chin.
Visible and invisible.
Chin trembling, his face shining.

"I was an orphan."

Yes, I know, dad.

"Did you know an orphan's dead parents
are able to attend the wedding?"

But dad, I'm not an orphan.

"Well, I just want you to know if you were,
we'd come anyway.
You know, your grandparents will be there too."

How will they manage that?

"What are you asking? They'll manage.
These are your grandparents:
Grandpa Hyman. Grandmother Bessie.
It's a tradition. Our Talmud says
if they have their bodies, they'll come with their bodies."

But they're dead.

"So, they'll come without."

3. Temple Washroom

"When a man unites with his wife,
God is between them.
I'm telling you: lovemaking is ceremony.
The Talmud says.
You, you're not holy, but your wife is.
With her
you go to a world outside the world."

So?

"So wash your hands before
not after.
Wash for the pure and holy bride."

But what about hygiene?

"How did I bring you up?
Shame on you.
The socks come off and you make love.
The Talmud says. And you make her happy.
Schtupp. Schtupp. Do you understand?
Forget hygiene!
This is the pure and holy bride."

Marriage #3

"Again? That's it.
This time marriage divorces you.
Just walk, walk now, keep walking.
Dr. Neusome's son eats and becomes sensible.
Horse radish, bagels, lox, cream cheese—
A *mensch*. Honorable.
But you, horseradish turns into what?
Divorce.
Bagels into divorce. Cream cheese
into divorce.
You know *schlemiel*? A *schlemiel* trips
and knocks down the *schlimazel*.
So which are you?
A love weasel, that's what you are.
He obtains a blessing, beautiful
young woman,
and out it comes, divorce.
With each divorce the *mensch* in you
gets split in two.
And there's no money in it.
Divide down the middle,
right down the middle,
Half of a half of a half...
The middle? This time
there is no middle.
And now the yoga...
The podiatrist's son walks now on his head.
Another blessing. Head over heels didn't work. So, *nu*,
now it's heels over head.
Yes, feet in the clouds, *ach*.
Such a blessing!
Fine, fine! Stand on your head if you like.
Some part of you at least will touch the ground."

Marriage #4

Palm Springs, Ca

"One, two, three... Shame
And more children than you can count.
Meshugge.
What have you learned? And now a fourth.
Everything in the world has meaning.
So, *nu*, tell me:
What's the meaning of this?
Earth, air, fire and foolishness...
The sun and the moon and the stars.
These I understand.
Hieroglyphics I understand.
But you! How many times does a foot marry a foot?
A man should tangle feet with one woman.
One pair of feet. One family. One home.
How many do you need?
'How's your son?' Mrs. Goldberg asks me.
'Fine, fine,' I say. 'He's getting married.'
'Ah, mazel tov, doctor!'
Three years later she says,
'So, how's the boy?'
'Fine, fine. He's married again.'
'Oi vay!' she says, 'children...'
She's been through it too.
People say it's human to want to put an end to things.
Well, not for those with their feet on the ground.
Look at your clever face in the mirror: Look,
look at yourself. Now count:
one face, one face you see, not four.
So, better that part of you with brains
should take off its socks and study feet. For that...
you don't need a mirror."

Feet Know the Way
to the Other World

One-Stop Foot Shop

"We walk with angels
and they are our feet.

"'Vibrating energy packets,'" he calls them. "'Bundles of soul
in a world of meat.' Early warning system—
dry skin and brittle nails;
feelings of numbness and cold;
these are symptoms; they mean something.
I see things physicians miss.

"All you have to do is open your eyes, just open your eyes,
and you'll see: seven-eighths of everything is invisible, a spirit
inside the spirit.
The soul is rooted in the foot.
As your friend Bly says, 'The soul longs to go down';
feet know the way to the other world,
that world where people are awake.
So do me a favor: dream me no dreams.
A dreamer is someone who's asleep.

"You know, the material world is infinite,
but boring infinite," he says, cigarette in hand,
little wings fluttering at his ankles.

"And women," he says, smacking his head,
"four times as many foot problems as men.
High heels are the culprit.

"I may be a podiatrist, but I know what I'm about:
feet. Feet don't lie,
don't cheat, don't kiss ass. Truth is,
peoples' feet are too good for them."

He Takes Me Back as a Patient

"So there they are, on a pedestal
your feet under lights.
More than you deserve,
you and those prima donnas.
Villains!" He points a finger.
"With normal people the socks come off
and the feet talk. But not these two.
Wise guys. Too good for diagnosis, huh?
Too good for arch supports? Is that it?
Your X-ray shows nothing. Ultra sound
nothing.
This is your last chance. This is it.
Weak ankles, feet out of alignment,
but there's something else.
I see it in your posture. You're holding back,
you and those feet of yours,
slippery feet,
meshugge feet,
feet like no one else in the family.
What's going on in there?" he asks.
"Wake up! Tell you what:
we're gonna have you walk around the office.
That's it. Head erect,
back straight.
No, no! Look at you, look at you: you call that walking?
On the ground, on the ground!
Dreamer! *Ach!* You're fired! Your mother was right.
You and those feet of yours are two of a kind."

God is a Pedestrian

Palm Springs, Ca

"Trust water, son, you can't go wrong with water.
See, and it's got dual arm rests,
multi-directional
massage jets,
pneumatic air switch,
a four-horsepower motor

"So, hold here, hold the grab bar—
get in, son. Take a ride on the plumbing express!

"Good for the feet,
good for the back.
Foot problems,
back problems,
they go together!"

I'm swept away.

Schlimazel! Hydrotherapy is your friend. Hold the grab bar,"
he yells.

"You want to know a secret?"

Please, dad, no philosophy.

"God is a pedestrian. God who is in heaven
is also a man, just like you and me."

And what about angels?

"I'm telling you, if they looked after their feet
they wouldn't need to fly."

Dad, you're nuts.

"Of course, everything is imagination. Rosicrucian says."

Rosicrucian?

"One saw the world in a grain of sand.
So, *nu?* I see it in a pair of feet."

No, dad, not feet again.

"Yes, feet. Feet. The sun and the moon and the stars.
Feet, feet are heaven, too, a heaven filled with stars.
Rosicrucian says. The world is a man and the light of the sun
and the stars is his body."

This is Rosicrucian?

"*Goyisheh kop!* Think! The two are one:
God exists in man so body is a form of soul.
Heal the soul and you heal the body.
Heal the foot and you heal the soul.
That world is in this world, and this world is in that."

So what are you saying, dad?
Maybe there is no 'other side.'

"What am I saying? Wake up!
This is the other side. You're there," he says,
handing me a towel, "right
here, right now. You're home."

Good News from the Other World

Palm Springs, Ca

"Dad, you're lookin' good," I say,
"like the fountain of youth."

His hands on my feet, grimacing, weary,
mercurial, wing-footed
eighty-year-old doctor.

Wears a denim shirt, bola tie,
turquoise and silver tip,
tanned, tennis-playing, macho…

"Making more money now,
more than in Skokie.
But you need arch supports," he says,
encasing my feet in plaster.

Damaged feet. Feet out of alignment.
Four-times married, forty-year-old feet.

"Well, good news from the other world," he says.

"Really?"

"The void is nothing but people's breath."

"So something survives?" I say,

"Feet survive. Feet and breath survive," he says,
"peoples' feet and peoples' breath."

"That *is* good news," I say.

"Don't mock me," he says.
"Do you know you still 'toe in'?

That your head 'pitches forward'?
You're past the halfway mark, son.
God is not altruistic, you know,
He doesn't make exceptions.
Of course things are dark and light at once."

Huh? Who *is* he? Whoever was my father?

Bloodied in some Russian pogrom.
Nixon-lover on the North Side of Chicago.
Blue denim, bola tie Republican.

Rosicrucian cowboy in the Promised Land.

Arch Supports—The Fitting

Greets me in the waiting room,
father with waxed,
five-eyelet shoes;
son, too, with spit-shine, five-eyelet shoes.
This is how I was brought up. I do it
to show respect.
Value your feet.

"Okay, un-sock those feet of yours," he says,
"let's see the felons."
I unlace my Florsheims: moist feet emerging
from their cave of leather.
Father holds up arch supports.
Curved knife in hand, he shakes his head
as he trims *just so.*

"Remind me. Why do I need these things?" I ask.
"Weak ankles and spine," he says. "Poor posture.
Your feet are fine.
Truth is, you should be more like your feet.
Robust, healthy feet.
Take a lesson from your feet," he says.
"Feet appreciate
custom made.
No Dr. Scholl's for these feet."

Slips in the inserts.
Arch support like a shoe
inside a shoe,
leather inside leather.

"Every step I take you're going to be there," I say.
"Every step," he says, "every step of the way."

God is in the Cracks

"Just a tiny crack separates this world
from the next, and you step over it
                        every day,
God is in the cracks."
Foot propped up, nurse hovering, phone ringing.
"Relax and breathe from your heels.
Now, that's breathing.
So, tell me, have you enrolled yet?"

"Enrolled?"

"In the Illinois College of Podiatry."

"Dad, I have a job. I teach."

"Ha! Well, I'm a man of the lower extremities."

"Dad, I'm forty-three."

"So what? I'm eighty. I knew you
before you began wearing shoes.
Too good for feet?" he asks.
"*I. Me. Mind:*
That's all I get from your poetry.
Your words lack feet. Forget the mind.
Mind is all over the place. There's no support.
You want me to be proud of you? Be a foot man.
Here, son," he says, handing me back my shoes,
"try walking in these.
Arch supports. Now there's a subject.
Some day you'll write about arch supports."

God's Podiatrist

Palm Springs, Ca

Corns, calluses, pain
in the joints of my toes.
Masked man in the half-light,
starched white jacket and pants,
shaking his head.

"Dad, what are you doing?"
"Re-fitting the supports.
What is it with you?" he asks,
"Why don't you respond?
I've never seen such feet.
With a word, the world came into being," he murmurs,
cigarette in hand.

"With you, with arch supports even
there are these feet that go nowhere.
Anyway, there's just one person,
God, God's body," he says.
"God has a body?" I ask.
"Of course he has a body, and feet.
"Feet?"
"*Feet*, of course feet.
You know he's not one to ask for help."
Throws me my shoes. "You're finished."
"Help?" I ask.
"It's the least I can do," he says.
"You're a podiatrist for God?" I ask.
"Varicose veins.
The aroma of infinity.
feet sparking,   feet an endless ocean,
                            feet made of music.
Of course I have to sort out foot from hallucination.
You can't treat a halo.
Don't look at me like that.
You're the one who doesn't respond to treatment.

God has feet like anyone else. You know it and I know it."
"I am that I am," I say.
"Says you," says my father.
"He is that he is and I'm his podiatrist.
What a son," he says.

V

After the Bypass

Palm Springs, Ca

1. In The Hospital

"Don't trust the world, son. It's filled
with holes. The best thing is to love…"

Love what, dad?

"Emptiness. I've been meaning to tell you:
There's a giant scroll suspended below the world
and it says this world
is made from letters and numbers
and every number is infinite.
Anyway, I'm invisible, son."

Dad, I can see you.

"You have two fathers,
one you can see,
one who looks like me;
and one you can't,
the father you'll never see.
The invisible *is* invisible,
but I need to make a living.
I'm a doctor, *nu?* What good is a doctor
if you can't see him?
Don't look at me like that. I'm still a Jew,
but some days all I see is Roses and Crosses.
Did you know the male body has nine holes in it?
Seven of those holes are in the head. So there you have it.
The world is a leaky boat, son."

187

2. Checking Out

Rosy cheeked father in a wheel chair.
He pulls out a toothpick. Makes little sucking noises
with his teeth. "Hospital food. Not as bad as they say."

Lights a cigarette.

"She's against it."

Who?

"Who do you think? She's against
the invisible."

Throws away the toothpick.

"I've fallen into a place where everything is music.
You know, if people could take a pill
and become invisible
there would be nobody in sight. It's true. The world
is made of love,
of our love for emptiness.
Ach, what the hell! Visible, invisible,
It's all the same.
Still, the world you go round thinking you can see
is filled with holes, and for every hole
in this world
there's a hole in the other. If you look,
you can see through the cracks.
I have a treasure now, it's true,
but no body.
And you, you *meshugge*, you have a body,
but no treasure.
You should take the year off. Spend some time
at the Invisible College."

3. Course Of Study

Lesson #1

"Stars ejaculate. That's how the world
came into being.
From sperm. The Sperm of the Stars."

Lesson #2

"There is no place empty of God.

"Darkness is a candle, too.

"So open the window in your chest.
Let the invisible fly in and out."

Lesson #3

"The invisible is more existent than all the visible things.
Talmud says.
Still, when you leave your body there's not much to stand on.
And there's a crack in the cosmic egg.
Truth is, this world is just one side of the nothing
that's on the other side."

Lesson #4

"Now I'll tell you about death.
Life has an eye to see, says Talmud,
but what do you think Death has?
Death is made of eyes,
made of eyes, dressed in eyes.
And when she comes, she comes with a knife
in her hands.
And you go through the wall and it's a flaming word.
Death is what happens when all you have left
is the life that was there all along.
But remember: you're still gonna need money
when you die."

Father,
One-Week Dead,
Strolling Up Palm Canyon Boulevard

Palm Springs, Ca

He wears a green surgical gown,
bristly white moustache and
a cheery, contented smile.

Shoe- and sock-shaped clouds above,
ghost-dog on a leash
gliding beside him.

"Smell that?" he says, lighting a Camel,
"that's it, son,
the aroma of the afterlife.

"Put someone in the ground
and you think he's gonna stop?
You're thinking the dead
shouldn't enjoy themselves?

"Anyway, my being dead counts for something;
listen to me, son. There's a saying:
You don't really belong to a place
until you bury your father there."

"WELCOME TO CALIFORNIA!" says Leopard Dog.
"HIS DEATH IS YOUR TICKET. TELL ME,
WHAT WERE YOU BEFORE?
A FLOATER, THAT'S WHAT YOU WERE."

"And there's a reason," Father says:
"a man needs a connection, someone on the inside.
As above, so below.
You've got an in in both worlds."

"THAT'S RIGHT. AND A DOG, TOO,"
says Dog.

Dog Door to Heaven

As spirit guide, whose job it was to guide his master into the next life and then to testify as to his master's goodness, dogs of intense devotion and loyalty were needed... As pets they have been affectionately raised as loyal companions... [and] as tools in the treatment of rheumatism.
—Ery Camara, "Looking at the Xolo," artnet.com

Dog:
"I can out-think, out-work, out-fight any dog
in that world or in this.
Woof fuckin' woof. I told you before, I'm here
to look after your father. Relax, dammit!
Besides, like the man said, 'Death is an illusion.'
Bow wow, bow wow!
Anyway, who else is gonna lie against him,
draw rheumatism from his body?
Leopard dog, that's who.
Even now he sleeps with his hands on me—
osteo-arthritis—
that need healing. Yeah, even in heaven.
Truth is, dogs are doctors, too.
Heaven, this 'other side,'
is one big hospital and, like I told you,
it's filled with dogs,
New Guinea Singing dogs, Xolos, Leopard dogs, dogs
that listen to you and protect you.
You think someone dies and God's gonna make them
whole again?
God's not perfect either. WOOF, WOOF!
People say 'Heaven is a place that cannot be found,'
but if you got a dog,
you can find it."

Dog, With Father, At Their Ease In Heaven

BOW WOW, BOW WOW. You know what heaven is?
Dogs, dogs and people,
dogs, everywhere, dogs—and people
who can't be without them.

Listen to me. You put a dog in this place
and you think he's gonna stop being a dog?
Or people? The dead don't change.
Whatever they were in life, they are now.
Look at your father over there, smoking;
you think because a person's dead, he's done?
Done? Done what?

And God? Sonny, He's not going to help you.

Anyway, everything oscillates
between is and is not.
On, off. On, off.
Yes, no. Yes, no.
Aristotle said it.
There's howling
and there's howling necessity.
There's the way things are
and the way they really are.

So, the dead don't want to hear you carrying on.
Mourn,
if you want to, but mourn with your mouth shut.
The dead don't want to hear it.
Forgive the dead for their mortality.
Forgive your father, Sonny, forgive him
for being dead.

A Man Needs A Place To Stand

"Snap out of it, son!
Yes, of course I'm dead,
but you think I've left the world?
Then how come you're talking to me?
Nu? ask yourself:
How is this possible? Listen to me:
There's more good news.
That's right: Death doesn't separate you from God.
This is a surprise? You were thinking
there's something to fear?

Anyway, wait till you die, son. You'll see.
We never entirely leave the world.
Ach, there's no 'there' to leave. There's hardly a 'here.'
And you, *nudnik*,
you just think you have a body.
Still, you can't chase the invisible.
Do that and you'll end up everywhere,
and then what?
A man needs a place to stand."

Life is its Own Afterlife

"Enough already. Mourn,
mourn all you want...
What good will it do?
Truth is, I feel great, son. Never better!

"So what if I'm invisible?
So what if I'm dead?
You don't need a body to be a *mensch*,
a man of substance.
Ach, but with a body at least
you've got some privacy.
Without a body you can't conceal anything.

"There's more, son,
and bad news for you.
This will surprise you—
when you die one of the first questions God asks is,
'Did you marry?'
Turns out after God created the world, the rest of the time
He spent making marriages.
So a couple, when they meet, it's *bashert*,
'it was meant to be.'
That's so... that's how
together they fulfill their destiny.
But divorce, that they don't allow.
So you won't be coming.

But thank God
for what you've got.
What are you missing? Not much. There is no afterlife,
not really.
That's right, son.
Life is its own afterlife."

From Beyond the Grave,
The Podiatrist Counsels His Son on Prayer

How to pray?
You're gonna need a password.
But not now. And you're gonna see
it's numbers, not words. Didn't I tell you: if it's got words,
it's not prayer, and it's not a password either.
So what if I'm dead? What does that matter?
You think you bury your father and that's the end?
Schmegegge! What are you thinking, that the living
have a monopoly on life?
Give the dead some credit.
I didn't just die, you know. Think of the preparation. A man
has to get himself ready. And what did I ask?
That you pay your respects. So light the *yizkor*,
light the candle. *Oi*!

Tear the clothes, rend the garment, I said, and that you did.
Point my feet toward the door, I said, and that you did.
God takes what He takes, son, and the body follows.
But prayer? Prayer? Where was the prayer?
Listen: God created us first the feet,
then the rest.

So? So we bow the head when we pray
to show respect. Cover the head,
where's your *yarmulke*? *Daven, daven*,
rock back and forth… Now ask:
'Who am I? Who *am* I?
What am I here for?'

These are the things you ask,
but this is not prayer.
It's what you need to know before you start.
Why are we here? We're here to mend the world.
That's it.

Just remember, God doesn't answer prayers.
So don't ask.
Don't ask for anything.
Shopping is shopping. Prayer is prayer.
Don't confuse the two.

This is a Father

Where are you going?
That you don't know, do you?
Yes, it's me. Who else would it be?
You think I don't see what you're up to?
Wait, I'm not finished.
He's in such a hurry to leave
but he doesn't know the address.
Walk, walk, that he knows, the easy part.
How will you end up?
You think I'm hard on you? I'm not hard enough.
Where do they come from,
smart guys like you?
And where do they go?
Head at one end, feet at another.
What kind of creature is this?
Meshuggener, a crazy man.
Two billion times in a lifetime it beats,
the heart.
And the brain, three and a quarter pounds,
200 billion neurons. And for what?
To walk. What, again!
Walks out on a wife.
Walks out on a child.
You I didn't walk out on.
For you I stayed—even now,
I may be dead, that's true,
but I'm not going anywhere.
This is a father.

New Poems

The Astronomer,
A Universe for Beginners

1. The Astronomer

Math Teacher: Sexual position when you are doing your partner and you yell out math problems like "What is the square root of 4?" and "What is 5+5?" You fuck him/her harder and harder to try to get her/him to get these simple problems wrong. —Urban Dictionary

"All galaxies in observable space
Recede from ours at the speed of light."
Navy vet undergrad, I follow
taking notes.
I'm with her, the astronomer.
"What's the square root of four?" she asks
all aglow,
Straddling me in the morning light. I'm imagining…
milky white and pinkish blue…
"Continuous creation out of nothing from nowhere".
She looks around the lecture hall. Points at me.
"What are we here for?"
"I dunno," I say, flustered. *"I mean…"*
"In the beginning there was nowhere," she says.
 "It all began with a ball of gas vibrating
And a great roaring," I scribble.
"The entire observable universe
would have been
about the size of a grain of sand."
Jesus, I'm thinking, now that's the way to begin a story!

But there's a complication.
"Our universe should be slowing down," she says,
"Instead, it's speeding up…
And galaxies are being forced further and further apart,
Stretching the very fabric of space."
Now she's riding me, harder, harder…
"The energy for that has to come from somewhere.
Dark, we call it, dark as in 'unknown,' dark… the dark forever."
O… Celeste, O Celeste!

2. Dark Matter

Collapsing The Deckchair: Sexual position in which the receiver lays (sic.) on his/her back, with waist at the edge of a bed. The giver stands next to the bed, with the receiver's legs on his/her shoulders. While penetrating, the giver may—at his/her discretion—lean forward to create extra tension... —Urban Dictionary

Celeste:
Teacher with a giant star chart, the whole of heaven in her arms.
"You'll need a telescope." Adjusts her Orion SyQuest...
 "Can you see it?" Points—to...
On my knees, squinting, I bow before the eyepiece.
"Cassiopeia," she announces, "the Seated Queen...
Cassiopeia in a deck chair."
'Up periscope! Go Bronco Buster,' I'm thinking,
'Missionary Position, Side Entry Constellation,
Puppet Master...'
"Legs up, legs up," I hear her say. "R U ready?"
What? What'd she say?
'C' student, I can barely keep up, don't know the math.
It's all darkness, a Universe for Beginners.
"Cassiopeia is at the edge of the Milky Way," she goes on.
"Five bright stars in the constellation form a rough 'W' in the sky.
Some see in this formation the shape of a chair.
"You over there, Mr. Sward" –gestures from her lectern—
"name and locate four others."
'Swing Time, Lazy Man, Belly Flop, Man Chair...' I say.
Digs in her heels beside her hips. I'm imagining...
"Align yourself," says Celeste. "Consider the angle—
That's it, that's it," *Figure 8 Swivel,*
The Lock and Pose, the Space Wheel...
The bulk of matter in the universe is dark," she says.
It's the invisible scaffolding for the formation of stars.
Dark matter," she goes on, " dark matter exerts a ghostly pull
On normal matter..."
Her ankles round my neck, I kiss her knees,
Leaning now, leaning forward
O... Celeste, Celesta, Ce-les-tas, Ce-leste

3. Space Wheel

Space Wheel: Sexual position that can only be performed effectively in outer space and less effectively while submerged underwater. The position is characterized by a standing doggy style without thrusting but rather with a circular motion of the female participant just like an airplane propeller." –Urban Dictionary

Celeste:
"Mass can consist of both visible matter, like stars,
And invisible dark matter," she says.
"Dark matter: a web-like structure…
Stretches throughout space," I scribble.
"Only because of the hidden,
does the visible world exist," she goes on.
What… whaat? I've lost her.
"Let me explain. Most of the universe seems to consist of nothing
we can see.
4% visible matter; 96% invisible…
And imagine: Dark energy makes up over 2/3 of the energy
In the universe, dark energy, some say,
That's what's pushing the universe apart." She holds up a chart.

We huddle together at the bottom of a pool,
Beanpole undergrad and the astronomer,
Clerestory windows above us. Imagining…
"You know, there's no escape," she says.
Gravity, *gravity* holds it all together."

"There is a way," I say, grasping her from behind,
As, weightless, *near* weightless,
she begins to rotate,
spinning
Faster and faster
Tight, black neoprene silver goggles and angel fins
Celeste, O Celeste, spiraling
Kissing first her neck, then her ankles, neck, ankles,
Auburn hair afloat and whirls
As still she turns, propeller, O propeller

And we rise heavenward from the tiled bottom
Beanpole and mermaid professor
Dawn's early light, rockets red glare
Lecture hall and telescopes lectern spinning in air
O Celeste, Celeste,

      O fairest of the fair

ii. In a World of No – The Dogs in my Life

The World According To Shelby

The world is going to the dogs
and I'm the dog the world is going to.
Shelby here, S-H-E-L-B-Y.
Lift your leg. What? You want my resume?
Sniff here. *Rrf, Rrf*...
If I can smell your ass
I know what you got up your sleeve.
Now shut up! Shut up and let me bark...

For starters, food has a way
of anchoring thought. I'll tell you that.
The stomach and the heart,
they're the same thing.
But I wanna know, after 10,000 years
of domestication,
what does it mean to be a dog anymore?
Of course it's true 90% of our genetic makeup
is the same as yours.
I read. I read shit like that.

You need. But you think I need? Need what?
An interspecies relationship?
As for sex, dogs don't do strap on's,
dogs don't do dongs. No three-ways.
Gimme a bow, gimme a wow,
 gimme a BOW WOW WOW.

No deep throat for dogs.
No twisted jelly shaft.
No pearl-beaded prolong ring.
Remember your WOOF WOOF
is connected to your BOW WOW.

Be cool. Love like war.
Winner is who stays longer.
You know, sometimes it's just good to hang out with your own kind.

In a World of No

…all that I cared for was the race of dogs,
that and nothing else… To whom but [dogs]
can one appeal in the wide and empty world?
—Franz Kafka

In a world of No,
dogs are a Yes.

Sixty-eight million dogs in America
and they understand
there is a fundamental human reaction
—to everything—,
and it's *No, No.*
Grrr! Dogs hate hearing shit like that.
People, it's all *No* and *No*
and *No.*

They look at a dog sometimes
and the dog is on its back, say,
on someone's lawn,
legs in the air,
rolling and bouncing…

'This is the hand I was dealt. I'm a dog,'
says the dog. 'It's not a problem.'
But people—
Look at me, Goddammit!
'I don't have time for this,' you're thinking.
'Something better is going to come later.'

No, no it won't. As Ram Dass says, This is all there is.
This is all you get.
'All knowledge, the totality
of all questions and answers,
is contained in the dog.'
Do you know who said that?
Kafka. That's right, Kafka.
Bow-wow, bow, wow. Bow, wow.
Bow-wow NOW.

Black Holes

Black holes lurk in the centers of most galaxies
belching x-rays as they swallow stray gas and stars.
—New York Times

Dogs know this shit,
the *crème de la crème* of *bow-wow.*
Astral barking, the music of the spheres.
Yeah, and they've seen the snapshots,
'black hole core samples,'
holes the Hubble found
billions of times the mass of the sun.
Bow-wow, bow-wow.
Look, dogs want answers too.
You don't think we have a hunger to know?
Not all dogs are rational,
but we're here for a reason.
We're here to take the lid off life.

So, which came first, galaxies
or the black holes inside them?
Bow-wow, bow-wow.
Just because you can't see something
doesn't mean it's not there.
Dogs know. Dogs knew from the beginning.
Once the universe was swaddled in gas
that blocked all light.
What else?
Humans use only 5 to 10% of their brain capacity;
90 to 95% goes unused.
Six hundred thousand years ago hominids first appeared
in Europe and Asia.
And that, from start to finish,
is just how long it took
to invent dog food.

Laika, Dog Astronaut

The more time passes, the more I'm sorry....
We did not learn enough
from the mission to justify the death of the dog.
—Russian scientist

Dogs into cosmonauts.
'Muttnik' they called her.
And 'Laika.' The name means *barker.*
Bow wow, 2,570 times around the earth,
then burned up on re-entry.
Imagine her now alive. "Comrade," she says,
"look in my eye. Tell me, what do you see?
Da! A dog biscuit 28 billion light years in diameter,
and it's floating in space. *Luminous splendor*
of the colorless light of emptiness.
That's the universe.
Bow wow, and you can hear it,
continuous song, the perfect but inaudible barking
of all the dogs that ever were.
Nyet, nyet! God isn't done creating, my friend.
The world is still coming into being."

Inter-Species Healing, A Specialty

So, what is consciousness?
75% of the brain consists of water,
the surface of the earth,-
75% water,
and a banana too, 75% water.

You and your *melancholia*. You know what it is, a brain?
A salty tissue and membrane soup. Woof fuckin' woof

I'm not the dog I was,
and you, well,
you're not the dog you were either.

But brains you got, three pounds, you people,
100 billion neurons,
1.6 pints of blood flow through the brain every minute.

Problem with you now is you live in the past.
You've got one frequency of oscillation,
we've got another. You know,
dogs are never "away," are they? But you, boss,
where are you?

Tell me, you think God is present in you one way
and in me another?

Look at me. If you have eyes,
you have feelings.

And what do they call it?
Inter-species healing.
You wanna get better? You're *getting* better.

Gimme Your Paw

We're comin' up to my birthday.
I'm seventy-seven—twenty-three more and I'll be a hundred!
So what's it all about, sixty-odd years of writing, scribbling?
I'm eye to eye with him, "Uncle Dog: The Poet at 9,"
first mutt I ever wrote about, the garbage man's dog.
Growing up in Chicago... *A doing, truckman's dog*
and not a simple child-dog
nor friend to man, but an uncle
traveling, and to himself—
and a bitch at every second can,
my first published poem. First book!

And I'm out now, out on my ass. The charge?
Muse-neglect. Dog betrayal.
Truth is, maybe I had it coming. I let him slip away.
Uncle Dog and I lookin' at one another.
And the dog has given notice.
It's been fifty years since I wrote those lines,
...sharp, high fox-
eared, cur-Ford truck-faced
with his pick of the bones...
So, what's today's dream?

"Gimme your paw," says Dog.
"Bad poet! Bad poet! What a mess! And five marriages.
All that scribbling.
Loss of nerve. Cowardice.
What'd you expect? What were you thinking?
Yeah, I know, we had our day,"
he says, and gives me back my hand.
Then it's like lookin' in the mirror,
and the "you" in the mirror walks out on you.

Head up, dog wings outstretched, circling, climbing,
ascends into heaven.

iii
Companion Animals

Companion Animals

The difference in mind between man and the higher animals, great as it is, certainly is one of degree and not of kind.
—Charles Darwin

Shelby:
"Ninety percent of our genetic makeup is the same as yours.
Twenty-two feet from your mouth to your anus,
And a brain the consistency of tofu.
It's alright, boss, dogs understand,
they know what it means to be human.
The doctor who said, 'The purpose of dogs
Is to stimulate the subcortical reward system',
That doctor needs a doctor.
Woof, woof fuckin' woof!
And if that's my purpose, what's yours?
And whose subcortical reward system we talkin' about?
And why should dogs have to stimulate anybody's anything?
The purpose of dogs is for you to walk
around after us with a little bag."

The Purpose of Dogs

The difference in mind between man and the higher animals, great as it is,
certainly is one of degree and not of kind.
—*Charles Darwin*

Ninety percent of our genetic makeup is the same as yours.
But you, my friend, twenty-two feet from your mouth to your anus.
It's all right, Boss, dogs understand,
They know what it means to be human.
Still, the doctor who said, 'The purpose of dogs
Is to stimulate the sub cortical reward system',
That doctor needs a doctor.
Woof, woof fuckin' woof!
The purpose of dogs is for you to walk around after us with a little bag.

Soul Catcher

Dogs got 220 million smell sensitive cells. Humans got 5 million. So, what is the source of all being? Boundlessness, a oneness where there is no two. There's some shit you're just born knowing. Now who you lookin' at? Face it, Boss, you're out of commission. Can't concentrate, can't think straight. You're impaired. You're not the dog you were. So tell me, if 90 percent of our genetic make up is the same as yours, if we're so much alike, is God present in a dog the same way He is in a human? All I know is there's more to shit than meets the eye. You lost your mind, Boss? Fine. I do retrieval. Some people got a Seeing Eye dog. You, you got a mutt that catches souls.

Gravitas

Hope is the feeling you have that the feeling you have isn't permanent.
—Jean Kerr

I can tell, Boss. You don't need to be a physician to know,
They're not firing right.
Those neurons in the frontal cortex of your brain.
Photophobic. Anhedonic.
You lived in color. Now you walk around in shades of gray.
Poor fucker. Can't think straight, can you, Boss?
You know, people think you got gravitas,
But all it really is,
is you're depressed.

The Soul Has Lost its Home

For lonely dogs with separation anxiety, Eli Lilly brought to market its
own drug Reconcile last year. The only difference between it and Prozac
is that Reconcile is chewable and tastes like beef.
—*New York Times*

Melancholia. You know, there's another name for it,
'Soul loss.' Symptoms include loss of appetite,
Insomnia,
biting and chasing your own tail.
Listen, dogs are people too. We know shit,
We know shit you don't even know is shit.
You got a mind. Dogs got a mind.
You lost yours?
You don't think dogs
Lose theirs?
Goofy, neurotic,
photophobic, anhedonic dogs.

So they get prescribed SSRI's which,
remember, says the New York *Times,*
Were first tested on dogs
Before being given to humans.
And why not? Melancholia. Tell me, Boss,
Is it worse for humans or for dogs?

Garden of Eden

Dogs tell the story:
In the Garden of Eden, when God threw out Adam,
All the other animals shunned him, except the dog.

*　　*　　*

The love between dog and man is idyllic.
Truth is, Boss, I'm the nearest you're ever gonna get to paradise.

*　　*　　*

To this day, when someone dies,
A dog goes along to testify on their behalf.

Dr. Sward's Cure for Melancholia

Melancholia

Father:
A grief without a pang...
—Coleridge

I'm the dead one, remember?
You think maybe now a little peace and quiet I deserve?
Thirty years in a casket.
Forest Lawn Cemetery. Palm Springs.
Well, I can't complain. It's not so bad!
But here you are... again. So, what is it this time?
You got a problem maybe with your foot? Your ankle?
You're limping.
California Foot and Ankle you should see.
No? You won't see a podiatrist?
Instead you drive ten hours to a graveyard. *Messhugener.*
And look at you, *schlepp, schlepp, schlepp,*
poor feet, poor posture, and the eyes—blank.
Thirty years I'm dead. But look at me, son. Never better. It's true.
That's right. You can die, son, and still—you can enjoy!
And you, *oi!* It used to be the living saw the ghosts of the dead.
Now it's the dead see the living.
So many ghosts!
And all the time sad. Once a mind these people had.
Once a mind *you* had. A little animal, even,
an animal you had inside you. Look at me, son.
I gave you breath, remember?
A little 'mood disorder' you call it?
The 'neurochemistry of emotion'? 'Pharmacotherapy'?
What kind of talk is that?

Maybe it's not your 'disorder' needs treatment,
maybe it's the treatment needs treatment.
You think the dead don't read? Melancholia. Black Dog. Depression.
Call it what you want. 14 million people a year got what you got.
One out of every ten people you see... and children too,
and twice as many women as men. *Oi!*
All your life... look at you, look at you... and now this.
Dogs even got an inner life. I got. Dogs got.
You think maybe a little joy you could use? *Oi!*
The problem with you is
you're not a dog.

A Face to Sadden God

When your father dies, you move to the head of the line.
This is a surprise? Truth is, I'm more alive than you think. Ready?
So, what is death? You learn to walk without your feet.
It's not so bad. Of course you're not your body.
You never were. But you're not your mind either.
Look at you, look at you—
With a face to sadden God.
You and your 'neurotransmitters.'
Mr. 'Mood Disorder.' Some people, when they got no—
there's a word. In you it's missing. *Nephesh*. 'Soul' it means!
Three years in Hebrew school and what did you learn?
No *Nephesh*, no Hebrew, no soul!
'Receptors' you got. 'Serotonin' you got. Zoloft. Paxil.
A pill to improve—what? A pill now you need,
but not an arch support? Me, I got a reason
to look the way I do. I'm dead.
But *Nephesh*, at least I got *Nephesh*. Listen...
There are three parts to the human soul. *Nephesh* is one:
Cobra soul. Snake soul. Even to be a reptile you need a soul.
It's true. So, where's your *Nephesh?*
Second soul is your mind. What wakes when you wake?
What thinks when you think? And where has it gone,
this mind you have lost?
Three: *Eudaimonia*, virtue, conscience.
            Eu, it means 'happy.' *Daimon*, 'spirit.' So, Goddammit,
where's your *eudaimonia?* This you need
to put your stink in order. Order you need to be happy!
Rabbi says, 'The soul needs a soul, and that soul needs a soul.
Three souls, one body. But you,
            where's the *Nephesh?* Where's the mind?
Of course I'm dead, but at least there's a ME to be dead.

In Heaven, Too, There Are Jews

Up here they got Soul Retrieval. Lucky for you, son,
lucky I'm dead.
That's right. I *know* some people.
In heaven, too, there are Jews. So, when did you last see—?
When did you last have— *Nephesh,* breath, soul?
Nephesh leaves, but *Nephesh*, it's true, you can bring back.
Rabbi says.
Meanwhile God says you need to gain a little weight.
Thinning hair. Poor posture. Look at you, look at you!
Happiness is missing. Confidence is missing.
Even what's missing is missing. And that soul of yours?
It's splintered, it's in pieces. It's in the Kabbalah.
Ruach, ruah, neshama... all gone. Your soul has left you.
So, without the invisible, son, there's no you.
What's to be done? A father dies and the son
becomes a zombie? Of course you miss me.
I'm dead. So what? I'm somewhere else.
This is a change? Goddammit, I've always been somewhere else.
Where does a father end? Where does a son begin?
Pay attention. Time to get the soul back. That's right.
But to retrieve a soul you need a soul."

The World is Broken

What? What do you think I am? I'm alive, I'm dead.
 Same as everyone else.
And you? You got a wife, she wants a divorce.
You got another wife. *She* wants a divorce.
Now *Eudaimonia* is gone. And you, you want a divorce from—who?
Yourself? So. One side of the self
is at war with the other?
The question is: Which side is which?
So divorce yourself and see what happens.
How many times do I have to say it?
You think the world is broken? Of course it's broken.
Enough! Enough! Thoughts have souls. Souls have souls.
Everything's a covering. And you, with that mug of yours,
what are you covering? Tell me,
What is a human being? What makes a person a person?

"Yes, you're broken. And yes, you're only visiting your life.
So, fine, fine. Why not live then as if you were still among the living?
Don't start eternity being depressed.

Surviving Death

What's to survive? Truth is, we all survive death.
But there has to be something there when you die.
What am I saying? A soul you need to retrieve a soul, Goddammit!
You got to start with the invisible to end with the invisible.
What do you think I am?
What do you think you are?
Neurochemicals you need to feel alive?
I may be dead, but *this* I don't need.
Biomolecules. Carbon. Hydrogen. Lipids.
Hormones. *Mishegoss*, nonsense! Wait'll you die. You'll see.
And you'll feel what you feel.
The neurochemicals of emotion?
I've said before: It's not your 'disorder' needs treatment, it's the
treatment needs treatment.
You think the living have a monopoly on life?
Of course we're all human. So: a son, you'll see, completes his
father, a son a father, a father a son. And you don't need to die,
you don't need to die to figure it out.

Soul Retrieval

He makes this simple thing, a soul.
But you, of even the invisible you make a mess.

Your soul has left you. *Shekinah* has left you.
Wives. Children. All gone. True. You are your home.
And your home has left you. And God,
you think He wants to be seen with you?

So, you *want* to die? Goddammit, you're already missing.
I may be dead, but I'm not missing.
What will dying—tell me, what will dying do for you?
What is it breaks when a man breaks down? What is it 'goes to pieces'?
The pieces. With a net I need to find you. First find. Inhale. Make clean.
Then breathe back into you. You know what it is, a soul?

All the pieces in one place.

Afterword
by Jack Foley

Uncle Dog Becomes A Bodhisattva:
An Introduction To Robert Sward

> *You don't look like a Canadian.*
> —Saul Bellow to Robert Sward

> *All I am really hungry for is everything.*
> —Robert Sward

Reminiscences from Cornell University, sixty years ago: I remember the eyes most of all: large, hazel-brown, luminous, kindly. And the manner: hesitant but pleasant. And the sense one had of a gentle, oddly elegant madness. He was tall: one thought he must look like Robert Lowell. And there was insight: he would stammer, but there were always ideas, intelligence, something worth listening to. And the oddity of the poems:

> I did not want to be old Mr.
> Garbage man, but uncle dog
> who rode sitting beside him.
>
> Uncle dog had always looked
> to me to be truck-strong
> wise-eyed, a cur-like Ford
>
> Of a dog. I did not want
> to be Mr. Garbage man because
> all he had was cans to do.

—from *Uncle Dog: The Poet At 9*

Robert Sward's career began in the late 1950s. He is a well-known poet, but he is not nearly as well-known as he should be. Sward's poems are often comic, but they are never *only* comic—or for that matter *only* serio-comic. X.J. Kennedy is a seriocomic poet of considerable capacity, but he is nothing like Sward who actually has more in common with W.B. Yeats, for whom the Trembling Of The Veil Of The Temple was a constant source of inspiration. Sward's poems are the result of a plunge into a never fully ironized, often hilarious sense of mysticism: they are the product of a restless, spiritually adventuresome sensibility masking itself as a stand-up comedian. Who but a mystic would write a passage like this— funny, but alive with the *via negativa*:

> The dodo is two feet high, and laughs.
> A parrot, swan-sized, pig- scale-legged
> bird. Neither parrot, nor pig—nor swan.
> Its beak is the beak of a parrot,
> a bare-cheeked, wholly beaked and speechless
> parrot. A bird incapable of
> anything—but laughter. And silence:
> a silence that is laughter—and fact.
> And a denial of fact (and bird).
> It is a sort of turkey, only
> not a turkey, not anything. —Not
> able to sing, not able to dance
> not able to fly.

—from *Dodo*

Sward describes himself as "Born on the Jewish North Side of Chicago, bar mitzvahed, sailor, amnesiac, university professor (Cornell, Iowa, Connecticut College), newspaper editor, food reviewer, father of five children, husband to four [now five] wives...."

Sward's mother died in 1948 at the age of 42; her last words were a request "to keep [Robert's] feet on the ground." The poet describes his podiatrist father as handsome—"a cross between Charlie Chaplin and Errol Flynn"—as well as "ambitious and hard-working," a "workaolic." By the time Sward wrote the poems collected in Rosicrucian In The Basement, the father has blossomed into a full-fledged eccentric, a visionary adrift in a world which doesn't comprehend him:

> "There are two worlds," he says lighting incense, "the seen
> and the unseen…
> This is my treasure," he says.

Like uncle dog, Sward's father is a comic version of the poet—but the terms have changed a little. Sward's father quotes Rilke (albeit unknowingly):

> "We of the here-and-now, pay our respects
> to the invisible.
> Your soul is a soul," he says, turning to me,
> "but body is a soul, too. As the poet says,
> 'we are the bees of the golden hive of the invisible.'"
> "What poet, Dad?"
> "The poet! Goddammit, the poet," he yells.

—from *Rosicrucian in the Basement*

It was only after his mother's death that the father became interested in Rosicrucianism and the world of the "invisible." Sward points out that the year his father became "a strict and devout" Rosicrucian was also the year that he, Robert, flunked algebra. The father's later amorous adventures with "Lenore" (shades of Poe) give the son the wonderful poem, "Lenore And The Leopard Dog." "I've told you before, dear," says the father, "God rewards you for kissing."

Like his father, Sward "lives in another world." But the young man is not so certain which world that is. When his father says, "As above, so below"—the famous formula attributed to Hermes Trismegistus—the son answers; "I'm not so sure." The word "below" is partly ironic since the podiatrist father is always talking about feet—"God has feet like anyone else. You know it and I know it"—and because the father carries out his rituals in the basement. Yet it is also a serious assertion about the relationship between the world of the senses and the "other" world. Sward's own impulses led him away from both Rosicrucianism and his family's

Judaism to the East. In "Prayer For My Mother," one of his most moving and accomplished poems, Sward is accused of being a "Jew who got away," a "sinner." But he also celebrates one of his meditation teachers, Swami Muktananda, "the biggest party animal of them all":

> Seven years I hung out with him,
> even flew to India, meditated
> in his cave
> chanting to
> scorpions, malaria mosquitoes
> so illumined they chanted back.

—from *The Biggest Party Animal Of Them All*

Sward writes, "I... was nicknamed 'Banjo Eyes,' after the singer Eddie Cantor. Friends joked about my name: "The Sward is mightier than the Sword." And because I had a zany imagination, I had only to say, 'Hey, I have an idea,' and other eight-year-olds would collapse laughing. I was regarded as an oddball, an outsider. I had few friends.'"

Robert Sward learned early that the comic, the "zany," was a mask by which one could assert oneself—through which one would be listened to. In his poems, the mask remains, but it is at the service of an essentially visionary impulse: "the vision, the life that it requires." The word "dream" haunts his work. Sward remains simultaneously "not so sure" and utterly certain:

> For two, maybe three, minutes
> I saw two worlds interpenetrating
>
> jewels into jewels,
> silver suns, electric whiteness,
>
> World 'A' and world 'B'
> one vibrating blue pearl,
>
> world like a skyful of blue suns
> *Whoosh! Whoosh! Whoosh!*

—from *The Biggest Party Animal Of Them All*

Neither in "this world" nor "the other," Chicago-born, a U.S. Navy veteran who served a stint in the combat zone in Korea (1952), Sward moved to Canada in 1969 to take up a position as Poet-in-Residence at the University of Victoria. While there he began to practice yoga, started a publishing company (Soft Press), met and for twelve years was married to a Canadian. Indeed, two of his children are Canadian citizens as is Sward himself—in truth, a citizen, at heart, of both countries. At once a Canadian *and* American poet, one with a foot in both worlds, Sward also inhabits an enormous in-between. It will come as no surprise to readers to find that his poems get at the moment of truth by being deeply unsettled, by refusing to rest in any particular other than the cosmic ambiguity of the wholly visionary and the wholly sensual. Past, present and future—and their tenses—assail him equally:

> As a teacher, I talk. That's present.
> For thirty years as a teacher, I talked. That's past.
>
> It may only be part time, but I will talk. That's future.

—from *Turning 60*

"During the late 1960s and early '70s," the poet writes, "American men arriving in Canada were assumed to be Vietnam War protestors, draft dodgers, or deserters… in 1969, I was a married, thirty-six-year-old, honorably discharged and decorated Korean War veteran. I was also the father of three children." Again the oddball, the outsider.

Sward taught at the University of Victoria from 1969 to 1973 and worked in Toronto from 1979 to 1985, when he returned to the United States. In January 1986, Sward moved from the mountains overlooking Monterey Bay (California) to Santa Cruz, a seismically active community of forty-five thousand people located seventy-five miles south of San Francisco. Another milestone.

Sward's friend, poet Morton Marcus remarked that "the physical and psychical environment [took] him by the tongue to new spiritual heights, which… slowed his responses to a meditative stillness and (surprisingly) eased him back into such closed forms as sonnets and villanelles." In

Santa Cruz, while earning a living as a freelance journalist, Sward served as food reviewer ("Mr. Taste Test") and, on one occasion, as the world's skinniest Santa Claus.

Sward's multiple marriages were by no means a source of pride: "I find each divorce hurts hurts hurts just as much, maybe more, than the one before... I have come to agree with Robert Graves, who says the act of love is a metaphor of spiritual togetherness, and if you perform the act of love with someone who means little to you, you're giving away something that belongs to the person you do love or might love. The act of love belongs to two people in the way that secrets are shared... Promiscuity seems forbidden to poets..."

In June, 1987 Sward met visual artist Gloria K. Alford (1928-2017) also originally from Chicago. Thirty years later Robert began work on a book-length poem, "Love Has Made Grief Absurd," a monologue in the voice of his late wife,

Robert Sward's poetry has undergone many shifts—including, as Marcus points out, the shift to closed forms—but its fundamental impulse seems not to have changed since I first came upon it in the early 60s. Outwardly "zany" and fanciful, it is inwardly serious, troubled and questioning. He has written over twenty books of poetry as well as some fiction and non-fiction; in the late 1980s he entered the Internet, poems a-flying. He has produced CDs. He once described himself as "a heat-seeking cocky mocky poetry missile... a low-down, self-involved dirty dog. Woof woof." He has noted how many of his poems have "to do with love, divorce, multiple marriage, aging, loss, and the challenge of bringing up children in a highly unstable world." He identifies strongly with strange and sometimes hostile animals.

What is sought in all this work is liberation, illumination—*it*. The joy of his writing is the joy of the quest. He has recently turned 87 and is producing work as fine as what he was producing sixty years ago. He has not grown up exactly, but he has grown. "These days," he says, "I'm paying more attention to Ben Franklin, 'Early to bed, early to rise, makes a man healthy, wealthy and wise.' and less to Blake with his lines about "the road of excess". From beyond the grave the poet's father counsels him, "Spend some time at the Invisible College."

When Robert Sward was a child his Rosicrucian father asked him, "So, Bobby, you too want to see God?" There is wisdom in Robert Sward's poetry, but it is the kind of wisdom we call "crazy." The final message of this work is not to transcend intense contradiction, (or "doubleness," as he would say), but to live deeply, even joyously, within it:

> I hardly unpack
> and get ready for this lifetime and it's time
> to move on to the next.

—from *Mr. Amnesia*

Jack Foley
Berkeley/Oakland, CA

Contemporary Authors, Volume 206, A Bio-Bibliographical Guide, Gale/Thomson, 2003

Appendix

Notes

Science of the Unseen

"The wise man sees in Self those that are alive and those that are dead." In his Introduction to *Patanjali's Aphorisms of Yoga*, translated by Shree Purohit Swami, W.B. Yeats quotes this line from the *Chandogya-Upanishad*.

"Spirit alone has value, Spirit has no value. Eternity expresses itself through contradictions."—W.B. Yeats
Yeats' book, *The Rose,* draws heavily on Rosicrucian symbolism. As a child, I had no inkling that the "Yeats" my father quoted was a poet. Up until the time I started college, Yeats, for me, was this Rosicrucian who wrote commentaries on texts my father brought into our previously Jewish home.

Rosy Cross Father. "We are the bees of the golden hive of the invisible." The phrase originates in a letter by Rainer Maria Rilke concerning his *Duino Elegies.*

Rilke writes ". . . It is our task to imprint this temporary, perishable earth into ourselves so deeply, so painfully and passionately, that its essence can rise again, 'invisibly,' inside us. We are the bees of the invisible. We wildly collect the honey of the visible, to store it in the great golden hive of the invisible. *The Elegies* show us at this work, the work of the continual conversion of the beloved visible and tangible world into the invisible vibrations and agitation of our own nature."

Lenore and the Leopard Dog. "There is man and woman and a third thing, too, in us," says the poet. Here I must credit the amazing Jelaluddin Rumi.

I am indebted to Paul Foster Case for his book, THE TRUE AND INVISIBLE ROSICRUCIAN ORDER, which provides an analysis of both the pre- and post-Mason Rosicrucians..." Case has defined

Rosicrucianism as "Christian Hermeticism allied with Kabbalah." Dad's journey from Orthodox Judaism to Rosicrucianism was not so great a stretch as I first imagined.

Rosicrucian. AMORC, Ancient Mystical Order Rosae Crucis.

Note to:
Rosicrucian In the Basement and *Heavenly Sex*

For my podiatrist father, Rosicrucianism is allied with *Kabbalah*—Jewish mysticism—and he began, following my mother's death in 1948, to put himself "on the right track for union with the Higher Self" (his words). A small businessman practicing in an ultra-conservative ~~middleclass~~ Chicago neighborhood he began thinking and talking like the New Age hippies, yogis and writers I became familiar with a decade or two later.

In section 4 ("Lenore Gets On Top") of "Lenore And The Leopard Dog," unable to recall my father's exact words, I found in the lines 'There is man and woman and a third thing, too, in us…' an approximation of what I felt him to be saying or trying to say. These lines are not mine. They are a borrowing from Jelaluddin Rumi, translated by Coleman Barks. A credit also appears on page 28 of the book *Heavenly Sex*. I am a student of Rumi and have been deeply influenced by him.

Dad never used the word *mandala*, but, for him, the American one-dollar bill included in its "pictures" much of what he thought one needed to know about the Self and how to survive in this world and find one's way to the next. In his mind, given its symbolism, the coin of our realm was designed by Rosicrucians (or Masons) like Benjamin Franklin.

With respect to "After The Bypass" and "A Man Needs A Place To Stand," I am thinking of W.B. Yeats. For Dad, Yeats was a Rosicrucian first and a poet second.

Bio Robert Sward:

Poet Laureate of Santa Cruz County, 2016-2018, Robert Sward has taught at Cornell University, the Iowa Writers' Workshop, and UC Santa Cruz. A Fulbright scholar and Guggenheim Fellow, he was chosen by Lucille Clifton to receive a Villa Montalvo Literary Arts Award.

His 30 books include: *Four Incarnations* (Coffee House Press), now in its second printing; *Heavenly Sex; The Collected Poems (1957-2004);* and THE TORONTO ISLANDS, a bestseller. Widely published in traditional literary magazines and anthologies, Sward has served as contributing editor to "Web Del Sol," "Blue Moon Review," and other online publications since 1995.

Born and raised in Chicago, Robert Sward served in the U.S. Navy in the combat zone during the Korean War (1951-1953) and later worked for CBC Radio and as book reviewer and feature writer for *The Toronto Star* and *The Globe & Mail.*

CPSIA information can be obtained
at www.ICGtesting.com
Printed in the USA
LVHW111652270322
714534LV00002B/291